W9-BXU-290

The Church and the Social Question

Franz H. Mueller

American Enterprise Institute for Public Policy Research
Washington and London

LIBRARY
COLBY-SAWYER COLLEGE
NEW LONDON, N.H. 03257

BX
1753
.M76
1984

Professor Mueller is Emeritus Professor of Economics at the college of St. Thomas in St. Paul, Minnesota. He is the author of *Heinrich Pesch: Sein Leben und Seine Lehre*, a biography of one of the architects of modern Catholic social thought who was also Mueller's teacher.

"The Church and the Social Question" originally appeared in Joseph N. Moody and Justus George Lawler, eds., *The Challenge of Mater and Magistra* (New York: Herder and Herder, 1963). It is reprinted by permission of the author and of Crossroads Publishing Company.

Library of Congress Cataloging in Publication Data

Mueller, Franz Hermann, 1900–
   The church and the social question.

   Includes index.
   1. Sociology, Christian (Catholic)   2. Capitalism—
Religious aspects—Catholic Church.   3. Church and social
problems—Catholic Church.   4. Catholic Church—Doctrines.
I. Title.
BX1753.M76   1984   261.8'09   84–18548
ISBN 0–8447–3567–1

1 3 5 7 9 10 8 6 4 2

AEI Studies 411

© 1984 by the American Enterprise Institute for Public Policy Research, Washington, D.C., and London. All rights reserved. No part of this publication may be used or reproduced in any manner whatsoever without permission in writing from the American Enterprise Institute except in the case of brief quotations embodied in news articles, critical articles, or reviews. The views expressed in the publications of the American Enterprise Institute are those of the authors and do not necessarily reflect the views of the staff, advisory panels, officers, or trustees of AEI.

"American Enterprise Institute" and ⟨ᴀᴇɪ⟩ are registered service marks of the American Enterprise Institute for Public Policy Research.

Printed in the United States of America

Contents

Sin and Social Disorder — The Need for Research — The Need for Historical Approach — Social Principles and Social Reality — Contingency, Counsel and Decision-making — Incertitude and Choice — Social Action by Law or by Faith? — "You are Christ's Body," the Church — The Church the Vital Principle of Society — Need for Lay Initiative — Relative Autonomy of the Cultural Spheres — The Church's Authority and the Social Apostolate — Catholic Social Action — Society and the Social Question — What Is "Society"? — From Status to Contract — The Genesis of Anomic Society — "Liberty" and "Equality" — Toward a New Concept of Status

The Three Stages of Modern Capitalism — Pre-Capitalism — Separating Forces of Capitalism — The Make-up of Economic Systems — The Principle of Sustenance — The Spirit of Capitalism — Origins of Capitalism — The Foster Role of the State — The Role of Mercantilism — The Church and Emerging Capitalism — Late Scholastics and the New Economy — Profits and Interest — Free Trade vs. Restraint of Trade — The Church and the Entrepreneurial Economy — The Concept of Status — Christian Humanism and Human Dignity

The Rise of Full Capitalism — Mercantilist Origins of Laissez Faire — "Revolutionary" Origins of Full Capitalism; The American

Revolution — Economic Implications of the French Revolution — The Agrarian Revolution — The Industrial Revolution — The Triad of Science, Engineering, and Business — The Rise of the Industrial Proletariat — The Idea of Competition — The Monetization and Mobilization of Life — Capitalistic Dynamics and Human Insecurity — Commercialism and Christianity — The Social Thought of Early-American Catholics — American Catholicism and Slavery — The Irish Laboring Poor and Catholic Colonization — The Church and American Labor — The Church and Georgism — Leo XIII and the Social Question — The Antecedents of Rerum Novarum — European Pioneers of Rerum Novarum — Panels and Study Circles — Factions and Schools of Social Thought — Divergent Views on the Role of Government — Other Issues — The "Roman Theses" — Rerum Novarum and the Schools of Social Thought — Leo XIII and the Social Function of Government — The Quintessence of Rerum Novarum — Recognition of Labor Unions — Catholic Union Leadership in America — European Allies — The Issue of Labor Legislation — The Other Side of the Coin — Corporatism or Meliorism — Protective Labor Legislation or Social Insurance? — Franz Hitze, the John Ryan of Germany — Church and State in Europe — The Church, Labor, and Citizenship in USA — Urban and Rural Catholicism in America — Rerum Novarum's Echo in America — John A. Ryan, Catholic Social Leader in the Making — John Ryan and the Central Verein — Kenkel and Ryan

LATE CAPITALISM AND CATHOLICISM

World War I Spawns Collectivism — The Waning of Capitalism — World War I and the End of Laissez Faire — Walther Rathenau, Symbol of the Great Change — Postwar German Corporatism and Father Pesch — Franz Hitze and Corporatism — Ryan's Postwar Meliorism — Ryan's Legislative Program — The "Bishops' Program" — Corporatist Implications — Ultimate Aims? — The Central Verein and the "Bishops' Program" — The "Program" and the "Pastoral" — The Pastoral Anticipates Vocational Group Order — "The Bishops Take Command" — The Bishops Warn of Paternalism — Wealth Concentration, Depression, and the Hierarchy — Corporatism vs. State Socialism

The American Enterprise Institute for Public Policy Research, established in 1943, is a nonpartisan, nonprofit research and educational organization supported by foundations, corporations, and the public at large. Its purpose is to assist policy makers, scholars, businessmen, the press, and the public by providing objective analysis of national and international issues. Views expressed in the institute's publications are those of the authors and do not necessarily reflect the views of the staff, advisory panels, officers, or trustees of AEI.

Council of Academic Advisers

Paul W. McCracken, *Chairman, Edmund Ezra Day University Professor of Business Administration, University of Michigan*

*Kenneth W. Dam, *Harold J. and Marion F. Green Professor of Law, University of Chicago*

Donald C. Hellmann, *Professor of Political Science and International Studies, University of Washington*

D. Gale Johnson, *Eliakim Hastings Moore Distinguished Service Professor of Economics and Chairman, Department of Economics, University of Chicago*

Robert A. Nisbet, *Adjunct Scholar, American Enterprise Institute*

Herbert Stein, *A. Willis Robertson Professor of Economics, University of Virginia*

Murray L. Weidenbaum, *Mallinckrodt Distinguished University Professor and Director, Center for the Study of American Business, Washington University*

James Q. Wilson, *Henry Lee Shattuck Professor of Government, Harvard University*

*On leave for government service.

Executive Committee

Richard B. Madden, *Chairman of the Board*

William J. Baroody, Jr., *President*

James G. Affleck

Willard C. Butcher

Paul F. Oreffice

Richard D. Wood

Tait Trussell,
  Vice President, Administration

Joseph J. Brady,
  Vice President, Development

Edward Styles, *Director of Publications*

Program Directors

Russell Chapin, *Legislative Analyses*

Denis P. Doyle, *Education Policy Studies*

Marvin Esch, *Seminars and Programs*

Thomas F. Johnson, *Economic Policy Studies*

Marvin H. Kosters,
  Government Regulation Studies

Jack A. Meyer, *Health Policy Studies*

Howard R. Penniman/Austin Ranney,
  Political and Social Processes

Robert J. Pranger, *International Programs*

Periodicals

AEI Economist, Herbert Stein,
  Editor

AEI Foreign Policy and Defense Review,
  Evron M. Kirkpatrick, Robert J.
  Pranger, and Harold H. Saunders,
  Editors

Public Opinion, Seymour Martin
  Lipset and Ben J. Wattenberg,
  Co-Editors; Everett Carll Ladd,
  Senior Editor; Karlyn H. Keene,
  Managing Editor

Regulation, Anne Brunsdale,
  Managing Editor

Foreword

Several years ago, under the leadership of my father, William J. Baroody, Sr., the American Enterprise Institute began to conduct occasional seminars in which top religious leaders and chief executive officers of major corporations could discuss their common problems at the intersection of religious values and the U.S. economy. More recently the American Enterprise Institute has cooperated with the U.S. Catholic bishops as they prepare for their Pastoral Letter on Catholic Social Teaching and the U.S. Economy, scheduled for completion in 1985.

The republication of *The Church and the Social Question*, a history of Catholic social thought by the distinguished scholar, Franz H. Mueller, Emeritus Professor of Economics at the College of St. Thomas in St. Paul, Minnesota, is a further contribution to that much-needed dialogue. It is the latest in a series of publications on religion and public policy pioneered by the American Enterprise Institute.

In 1976, seeing the urgent need for studies of religion and public policy, my father was the first president of a major think tank to devise a center for Philosophy, Religion, and Public Policy. In the next year we together invited Michael Novak to head this program. The present book has been published under the auspices of that program.

In 1978, 1979, and 1980, during summer institutes on religion and economics, jointly sponsored by the Department of Religion at Syracuse University and by AEI, Dr. Mueller's authoritative history of Catholic social thought, although long out of print, proved extremely useful. We proudly bring the book back to public attention now as volume 1 of a two-part study. We have further commissioned Dr. Mueller to complete volume 2 (forthcoming) to carry this important work through the years 1962–1982.

It is a pleasure to participate in bringing to the public what has been judged a small classic. We hope that it, like all the work of AEI, will contribute to that free competition of ideas which is the lifeblood of a free society.

WILLIAM J. BAROODY, JR.
President
American Enterprise Institute

Introduction
Michael Novak

Throughout the coming two decades, Catholic social thought on economic questions is bound to receive increasing media exposure. First, in 1985 the Catholic bishops of the United States will issue a pastoral letter on the U.S. economy. Second, the Vatican Commission on Justice and Peace and the pope himself are likely to speak out increasingly on the economic necessities of the less-developed countries, in which a majority of the world's Catholics now live. Third, the very success of the relatively few democratic capitalist political economies around the world makes it possible to turn to them, in their success, for much-needed assistance of every kind. It is part of a Jewish-Christian and humanistic culture to regard all human beings as brothers and sisters and in their necessities to come to their assistance as best one can.

Two centuries ago, confronted by the almost universal poverty of nations, Adam Smith tried to imagine a world in which the sustained creation of wealth to alleviate human misery might be achieved. He imagined a world of universal development, of international interdependence, of relative concord and reliable law, within which poverty, ignorance, ill-health, and misery would no longer find excuse.

For various reasons, this vast creative effort on the part of a new art and science called political economy was mixed with certain fairly broad philosophical and moral principles. In several of its varieties on the European continent, particularly in France, Germany, and Italy, the new "liberal" world view seemed to the popes to be antireligious and, often enough, anti-Catholic. It was certainly a break not only with the *ancien régime* but also with the village- and guild-oriented world view of medieval Catholic cultures. To abbreviate a long tale, the popes often found themselves in bitter opposition to the Continental liberals and, at least by analogy, with what they understood of Anglo-American liberalism.

7

Clearly, the popes opposed liberalism *as an ideology*, which they considered too materialistic, exaggeratedly individualistic, and—perhaps most of all—too burdensome on the families of those former serfs and peasants who streamed, defenseless, to the new industrial towns and cities.

Without question, the new liberal societies did engender a new ethos and a new ethic, not in all ways akin to the traditional ethos of the preceding era. Bitter misunderstandings were inevitable. Many of the populations most loyal to Rome, for example, were predominantly rural and aristocratic. As Lester K. Little shows in *Religious Poverty and the Profit Economy in Medieval Europe* (Cornell, 1978), the medieval Church, led by the Franciscans and the Dominicans, had slowly been developing a new urban lay spirituality of commerce and fledgling industry; but this slow process was rapidly overtaken by events.

As F. S. Nitti showed in *Catholic Socialism* (which first appeared in Italy in 1890 and which is said to have influenced Leo XIII's *Rerum Novarum* of 1891), the strong inherited *social* sense of Catholics, especially in France and Germany, led to various alternatives to individualistic liberalism, on the one hand, and to atheistic forms of socialism and communism, on the other.

The ambivalent relation of Catholic social thought to liberalism grew out of a long and complex struggle from the days just before the French Revolution. The pope still presided over the papal states. The struggle by liberals to liberate the papal states—specifically, by Mazzini, Garibaldi, Cavour, and Napoleon—was bitter and often quite less than moral. Liberalism came to have a bad odor in Rome.

Nonetheless, it was in Germany, above all, that the *intellectual* battle between Catholic social thought and liberalism was most systematically fought out. This was, in part, because Germany was the latest of the major Northern states to become unified, to experience industrialization, and to feel the full brunt of already formed ideologies: liberalism, taken mainly from France, and—through two of its native sons, Ferdinand Lassalle and Karl Marx—socialism and communism as well. Furthermore, German Catholicism was vigorous, both in constituting a large fraction of Germany's population and in sustaining the intellectual life of its leaders. Unlike France, whose Catholic institutions of higher learning had been destroyed under the Revolution, and unlike Italy, whose traditional anticlericalism inhibited a vigorous Catholic intellectual life outside clerical circles, Germany had been, since at least 1848, a citadel of the encounter of intellectual Catholicism and modernity.

Thus, when many years ago I first read Franz Mueller's short history of Catholic social thought, I felt myself in the hands of a master. An immigrant to the United States from Germany, Professor Mueller had come in his earliest days under the influence of one of the greatest philosophers of economics in Catholic history, the esteemed Jesuit, Heinrich Pesch (1854–1926). The young Mueller became restless under the contrary tugs of a socialism that seemed to yield too much to the state (and in practice to atheism as well) and a liberalism that seemed to be both based upon a faulty philosophy of the individual and too heedless of social justice. He became part of an active circle of German scholars whose formative influence upon papal social thought has been immense and unrivaled. One of their number, the younger Jesuit, Oswald v. Nell-Breuning, S.J., in collaboration with G. Gundlach, S.J., was specifically chosen by Pius XI to draft the second most important document in papal social thought (the first being *Rerum Novarum*), the famous *Quadragesimo Anno* (1931). Indeed, Nell-Breuning was soon thereafter to write the authoritative commentary on that letter, which appeared in English as *Reorganization of the Social Economy* (Milwaukee, 1936). Mueller himself has written a short biography of Heinrich Pesch which has, alas, appeared only in German.

Professor Mueller's short history of Catholic social thought is, therefore, the work of a scholar who has given almost an entire lifetime to its study, in the very centers of activity and in the company of those colleagues who were its most influential pioneers. It could only have come from one with the insight and the sense of nuance enjoyed by having been, in a sense, "present at the creation."

Thus Professor Mueller's work is especially important just at this time. The American Catholic bishops inherit a body of social teaching that is quite critical of liberalism—a movement which Rome has understood in a special Continental way—and Professor Mueller grew up within an influential part of this antiliberal tradition in Germany. Professor Mueller took part in the famous "Koenigswinter Study Circle," two of whose members were summoned to Rome to help draft *Quadragesimo Anno*. Then, in 1934, he was fired from his post at the University of Cologne by the Nazis. After a year in Britain he accepted a professorship in the United States, where he has dwelt ever since. Professor Mueller knows well both the advantages of liberal societies and the traditional skepticism about them characteristic of Catholic social thought.

Thus readers who wish to grasp more fully the cultural force of traditional Catholic social thought will find it expressed here clearly and intelligently. Few if any Americans catch its precise European flavor as Mueller has; few if any Europeans share Mueller's critical distance from the European context. This work, in short, is like a bridge between cultures—and between two different ways of perceiving the liberal society. I hope that American Catholic thinkers will follow up this study by a full account of how a liberal society such as that of the United States differs from Rome's conception of liberalism.

Because of Professor Mueller's unique point of view, I suggested to him when we met in 1979 that putting this short history into book form would serve an important historical function. I also encouraged him to carry the story forward from the beginning of the 1960s, where he had left it. Although limited in his daily strength by his advanced years, Dr. Mueller kindly agreed to do so with the help of his learned wife, Therese.

The exigencies of publishing have decreed that we could best proceed by publishing the present text as volume 1 of a projected two-volume set. When Professor Mueller completes volume 2, covering the years from 1960 to the present, we will have the privilege of publishing it as well. These two volumes together promise to be the best statement of the history of modern Catholic social thought in English and should be influential for years to come. We are privileged to be allowed to bring them before the public.

Working with Professor Mueller, meanwhile, has been a joy. His seriousness of purpose, independence of mind, attention to detail, and sparkling sense of humor are precious gifts. I think I have never known anyone who could get so many words—and so much important detail—on a single postal card, many of which figure importantly in the files guiding this publication to press. He has been unfailingly cooperative, generous, and watchful.

I believe the readers of this book will sense his character and warmth of mind, as they will be grateful for his clarity and careful illumination of basic points. There is no better short summary and introduction to these important historical materials. All who turn to the book will long be in Professor Mueller's debt.

The Church and the Social Question

Franz H. Mueller

THE SOCIAL MISSION OF THE CHURCH

THE history of civilization is a history of social problems and social questions. Though it would be an unwarranted simplification to reduce human history, as Karl Marx did, to a history of class struggles and social conflict, there is no denying that from time immemorial mankind has been plagued almost continuously by more or less severe disturbances of the structure or the functions of society. Along with these disorders there have, gratifyingly, always been attempts to find both the causes of and the remedies for them.

Sin and Social Disorder

The Christian is conscious of the fact that in the final analysis any malfunctioning and any decline of the social order is caused by original sin or, rather, by the wounds which original sin has inflicted upon human nature.[1] This awareness of the fact that man's general propensity, after the fall, has been toward uncontrolled self-love, and that this propensity is at the bottom of all social frictions, frustrations, and maladjustments, is basic to the understanding of the fundamentally moral and religious nature of any disorganization, and thus also of any reorganization, of society.

The Need for Research

However, it would be a grave misconception of this basic truth to interpret it to mean that there is therefore no sense in any attempt to trace and locate specific and proximate causes of a breakdown of the social order as a whole, or of any particular area of social interaction. Moral theology and ethics are not meant to

13

substitute for the empirical sciences of history, economics, and sociology. There is, ordinarily, no "short circuit" between the natural and the supernatural. God, the uncreated First Cause, operates through the medium of the secondary or created efficient causes. St. Thomas tells us that neglecting and disregarding the *causae secundae*, that is, ascribing everything directly to supernatural causes or to a special intervention of God, amounts to a derogation of the divine order of the universe. The Creator, from the abundance of his own goodness, has conferred upon his creatures not only their being but also their causality, i.e., their ability to be, in a certain sense, causes in their own right.[2]

The Need for Historical Approach

Those who, in the words of St. Thomas,[3] withdraw from or deny natural things their proper operation, consequently tend to be ahistorical in their approach to temporal problems such as those of the societal order. Already Augustine in his theology of history, the *City of God*, took to task those who denied historical progression and who taught that one and the same world is perpetually resolved into its elements and renewed at the conclusion of fixed cycles in which all things come around again to the same order and form as at first.[4] He could have referred to the cosmological cyclicism of the Eleatics (Sixth Century B.C.) who taught that what is must always have been and must always be and that there is nothing real in what appears to the senses to be motion and change. This skepticism toward individuation, toward the "here and now" was typical of Greek philosophy in general.[5] This is hardly surprising because the pagan lives exclusively in the realm of nature which is characterized by perennial repetition.[6] The Christian, however, recognizes the historical creativity of the human person and, therefore, realizes that history, instead of being repetitive, is essentially creative. Windelband saw clearly that, notwithstanding the far-reaching influence of Greek thought on the philosophy of the Christians, Christianity "found from the beginning the essence of the moving forces of the world in the experiences of personalities." "In contrast with the naturalistic conceptions of Greek thought," Windelband tells us, Christianity conceives of history "as a realm of free acts of personalities, taking place but once, and the character of these acts, in keeping with

14

the entire consciousness of the time, is of essentially religious significance." Among the Christians there arose the completely new thought that not only nature has its *telos* but "that the course of events in human life also has a purposeful meaning as a whole. The teleology of history (even) becomes raised above that of Nature, and although Christian thinkers hardly contemplated as yet a possible relationship, both in fact and in concept, between the two, there are indications that the former was looked upon as a kind of prelude to the latter." Windelband anticipates the approach of the more recent sociology of knowledge by pointing out that it took a universal civilization such as that of the Roman Empire (as contrasted with the "insular" civilization of the Greek city states) to make man conscious of history. Actually, Augustine's *City of God*, can hardly be thought of without the fall of Rome. Ever since the advent of Christianity, "the human race has gained the consciousness of the unity of its historical connection and regards the *history of its salvation* as the measure of all finite things."[7]

Social Principles and Social Reality

It is exactly in connection with her social encyclicals that the Church has demonstrated her genuine concern about the situational and temporal problems which Christians face as contemporaneous members of "secular" society. Addressing herself to men of all eras and areas, she does indeed put great emphasis on the common nature of these problems. She does not claim, however, that her general principles answer directly concrete remedial and constructive needs. Like St. Thomas, who over and over again stresses the need for specific determination of what is good and just under the prevailing circumstances, the Church calls upon her members to make their own prudential decisions within the framework of what is generally demanded by faith and morals. She marks the boundaries and puts up signposts, but she does not ordinarily prescribe the route to be taken to the goal in question. Frequently, there is a great variety of possible and legitimate routes leading to the same end. Instead of taking the Christian by his hand, as it were, to show him the way, the Church expects her mature members to examine the various operational possibilities, compare probabilities of success, and then make their own con-

15

scientious choices. Pope John XXIII speaks of the three stages by which social principles are applied: observation, judgment, action. He acknowledges, however, that "when it comes to reducing these teachings to action there may arise even among sincere Catholics differences of opinion."[8] This calls for mutual consultation and for cooperation, and, if need be, for authoritative decision.

Contingency, Counsel, and Decision-making

"There is much uncertainty," St. Thomas tells us, "in things to be done; because actions are concerned with contingent singulars, which, by reason of their vicissitude, are uncertain." "In things doubtful and uncertain," he goes on to say, "the mind [ratio] does not pronounce judgment without previous inquiry: wherefore the mind [ratio] must of necessity institute an inquiry before deciding on the objects of choice; and this inquiry is called counsel." "Counsel properly implies a conference held between several . . . Now we must take note that in contingent particular cases, in order that anything be known for certain, it is necessary to take several conditions or circumstances into consideration, which it is not easy for one to consider, but are considered by several with greater certainty; since what one takes note of, escapes the notice of another . . ." Typically in the Greek philosophical tradition, Thomas feels that "the knowledge of the truth in such matters does not rank so high as to be desirable of itself, as is that of things universal and necessary." Nevertheless, he does acknowledge that such knowledge is needed "because it is useful toward action, since actions bear on things singular and contingent."[9]

The late philosopher Yves Simon has shown convincingly that when common counsel does not lead to agreement and unity of action, authoritative decision may be needed, especially if the common good is at stake. It is exactly because men are unable to overcome the mysteries of contingency that even virtuous men, perfectly unanimous as to the end to be achieved, may—without quarrel—differ as to the means to be used to attain the goal in question. What is this "contingency" which the philosophers refer to? It is the simple fact that all created being is not "necessary" being: it may or it may not be or it may be other than it is. God alone "is"—everything else depends on him and is, therefore, changeable and perishable in being, or is being which can fail in its proper or intended effect.[10] That is why men are unable to foresee the future with certainty. That is why not even the wisest member of a community could ever demonstrate beforehand and beyond any doubt, "that this or that practical judgment, to be taken as a rule for . . . common action, is the best possible one."[11]

Incertitude and Choice

In the purely physical realm we are justified, even obliged, to assume that, ordinarily, the God-given laws of nature will operate. In the realm of human, especially social, action we must also take into account man's free will and his susceptibility to error. On the basis of our knowledge of human nature and on that of statistically recorded experience we may assume likely behavior and probable results; but the variety of possible choices precludes any certainty of prediction.

Considerable progress has been made in the behavioral sciences in eliminating the exceptional, in determining propensities and trends, and in calculating the chances that a given social action will achieve certain results. However, unless we deny the personal nature of man, we must admit essentially insuperable limits to the exactitude and certitude of the social sciences. This granted, it should not be difficult to see that there must of necessity be even less certitude in the field of social action or social policy. The economist is on relatively safe ground when he analyses a fact situation and demonstrates, perhaps with mathematical symbols, why, in all likelihood, under the circumstances in question, certain devices, procedures, policies, or plans proved themselves to be "operational" or why some did not. But when he proposes certain measures, sets certain goals, submits certain programs, he moves from the area of analytical statements and science to that of moral philosophy, history, and prudential decision and action. Here he faces entirely new and unpredictable situations, essentially unique and unrenewable, where the outcome of human action is a matter of probability, never one of certainty.

Such situations represent the "Rhodus" where the Christian has to prove himself, where he must take the leap. Neither the encyclicals, nor St. Thomas' theological summa, nor any catechism of Christian social principles can tell him exactly what he has to do under these specific circumstances. The Church will show him

17

the directions, but she will not and cannot relieve him of that responsibility which is the sequel of the "law of freedom" (Jas. 1:25), "the liberty which we enjoy in Christ Jesus" (Gal. 2:4). Thus he cannot expect the Church to give him directives, that is, practical instructions about methods and devices to be used at a concrete occasion. The Church, Pius XII once said, provides the lighthouses or presents the lighthouse to enable the mariner to inform himself about the position of his ship relative to the shore, the reefs, and the harbor; but, like the lighthouse man, she does not order the navigator where to go, here and now, nor does she chart the course to his destination.[12] Like a map which designates the location of the ports, of the points of danger, and the various depths of the sea, or like the compass which indicates directions, Catholic social principles give, as it were, the points of departure and destination and enable the traveler to find his bearings, but they do not relieve him of his duty to seek his own course of action, to do the timing and the steering, and to decide what to do in the case of interference or miscalculation.

Social Action by Law or by Faith?

The eagerness with which many Catholics expect Rome to "legislate" and minutely direct social action seems to be indicative of a basic—and disquieting—misconception of the New Covenant, which, as St. James tells us in his epistle (1:25), is really the law of perfect freedom. St. Paul does not tire of expounding the wondrous beauty of this, the New Law, which Augustine epitomizes in the comforting and reassuring words: "Love and do what thou wilt."[13] Yet many Christians persist in fearfully holding on to the legalism of the Old Testament, reducing the Church, which has always been and always will be a loving mother and a wise teacher, to a governess and a tutor, or to a matron and a monitor (cf. Gal. 3:25). The true Christian lives and acts ex fide, not ex lege, which is to say that it is not merely the law, the natural law included, which determines his actions but his whole being as a believer in, and faithful follower of, Christ.[14] It is indeed "the omission of special dictates for moral behavior" which distinguishes the New Covenant from the Old.[15] The Old Law, Thomas tells us, "determined many things and left but little to be determined by human freedom."[16] Now, *post Christum natum*, "the faith that finds expression in love is all that matters" (Gal. 5:6). As Paul tells us, "we are no longer to be minors [*parvuli*]," but mature Christians, challenged and encouraged "to share in the glorious freedom of God's sons" (Eph. 4:14; Rom. 8:21).

It goes without saying that this freedom does not excuse any exaggerated spiritualism or spurious supernaturalism. While it is true that faith without charity is like an empty noise (Cor. 13:1), and that it is through deeds that faith is realized (Jas. 2:22), it is equally true that charity without justice is inconceivable. It is significant that where Paul states that he who loves his neighbor has done all that the law demands (Rom. 13:9), he expressly lists some of the precepts commanded by justice as included in this law. Again, it is Paul who approvingly refers to the adherence of the Gentiles to the natural law (Rom. 2.14).

In one of the opening paragraphs of *Quadragesimo anno*, Pope Pius XI stressed the fact that it can never be "the task of charity to make amendments for the open violation of justice . . ." And in another place of the same encyclical (137) he says that clearly "charity cannot take the place of justice unfairly withheld." But while, in a sense, charity presupposes justice, actually nobody can be truly just who knows no love of neighbor; and even justice, in the Christian dispensation, is not of the law but of the faith (Phil. 3:9). For, "if we can be justified through the law, then Christ's death was in vain" (Gal. 2:21).

"You are Christ's Body," the Church

Paradoxically, complaints about a failure of the Church to give "concrete" answers to society's existential problems often come from the very same quarters that express concern about a lack of opportunities for, and of encouragement of, lay initiative in the Church. They and numerous other well-intentioned Catholics speak of the Church as if they are not part of it, that is to say, as if the Church were an extraneous organization; forgetting that the Church is a moral body that consists of head *and* members, they resemble those who identify the government with the state. It should be obvious, however, that the Church, thought of as the visible union of all the faithful under Christ and his vicar, is not, as such, an agency of social reform. Since in this life

19

man's spiritual soul operates through the medium of his material body, the Church does, however, take a deep interest in the physical welfare not only of her members but of all mankind. If, as Pius XI has stated in *Quadragesimo anno* (130, 132), as a consequence of a defection from Christian principles in social and economic matters, there are "vast numbers of men who can only under greatest difficulties accomplish the one thing necessary, namely their salvation," the Church cannot possibly remain indifferent. She must exhort, inspire, and—if need be—even look for practical remedies. But the immediate and proper purpose of the Church is clearly not institutional reform and the advancement of the material standard of living, but the sanctification of men through the teaching of the truths of religion and the administration of the sacraments.[17] The redemptive function of the Church does, of course, extend to society also. However, the establishment of the kingdom of Christ in the world is primarily the result of the perfection of the members of his Mystical Body through grace and their cooperation with it. It is thus, as Pope John XXIII has pointed out (*Mater et Magistra*, 221, 226, *et passim*), not so much through the pronouncement, reiteration, and profession of timeless principles that society is restored to Christ (Eph. 1:10), as it is through "timely" deeds, that is, through the leavening process of Christian living—*ex fide ad fidem* (by faith for the faith)—in society.

The Church the Vital Principle of Society

This mission of the Church, therefore, is by no means restricted to the sanctification of individual souls. She is indeed, as Pius XII once expressed it, the vital principle of society. But this vitalizing and formative effect does not come primarily from social doctrine or the authoritative pronouncement of social principles. Furthermore, there is no perennial ideal Catholic social system to be realized throughout the world and to last to the end of times. When Pius XII spoke of the permeating social dynamics of the Church, he had in mind the Church as a community of "builders" engaged in the construction of human society: "the community of those who, under the supernatural influence of grace, in the harmonious development of all human inclinations and energies build the mighty structure of human society." What is particularly important is the fact that the Holy Father makes it clear that he does *not* speak merely of the *ecclesia docens*, the pope and the bishops, but primarily of the *ecclesia discens*, the faithful, and more correctly, the lay people, who, he says, stand in the front line of the Church militant.

Need for Lay Initiative

"A Christian-social movement," says Oswald von Nell-Breuning, S.J., "must receive its direction from the Vicar of Jesus Christ; but it can become effective only as a powerful and broad movement of the laity. Without the cooperation [*Einsatz*] of the laity in all areas of social action—the term "social" here taken in the widest sense of the word—the pope would be a commander in chief without an army. This army, however, can have striking power only if the lay people do not patiently and resignedly wait for orders from the high command [*Führung*] but on their own initiative and their own responsibility proceed to act; if it is not merely a stolidly obedient body of soldiers, but provides courageous and determined leadership that unburdens ecclesiastical authorities of everything of which they could possibly be relieved."[18]

Commenting on the truly remarkable statements of Pius XII in his allocution of February 1946, Father von Nell says that they would be meaningless and ineffective unless the faithful at long last grasp the truth that, as the Holy Father said in so many words, "they *are* the Church," the community of the faithful on earth united under the guidance of the common head, the pope and, in union with him, the bishops.[19]

If we see the Church under *this* aspect, Pius XII said, that is, not merely as the papal government, but as the *ecclesia*, the whole body, composed of head *and* members, it should be obvious that she can never cut herself off, retiring to her sacristies, as it were, "and thus desert her divinely provident mission of forming the whole man, and thereby collaborating without rest in the construction and solid foundation of society."[20] The type of social action that Pius XII demands contains all that is essential in the lay apostolate, in Catholic Action, and in the Christopher movement, and more than that: a challenge to the religious maturity of the rank and file and their lay leaders who, in the sacrament of

21

confirmation received the Holy Spirit to give them the strength and the insight to find *for themselves* Christian solutions to the many problems that present themselves to the Church at large at all times and in all situations of public and private life. With every *Ite, missa est* this challenge is renewed and repeated as an earnest and urgent appeal to all the faithful to give testimony of their belief, in the world and in the market place.[21]

Relative Autonomy of the Cultural Spheres

This may explain why the Church has refrained for so long— or so it seems—from defining her position in regard to the social "isms" and errors of modern times. If by "the Church" we mean the papacy, we may assume that one of the main reasons for her reluctance to intervene has been her respect for the moral maturity of her members, especially those of the laity who are in a position of influence. Unfortunately, just as people have come to expect constant direction and aid from the government of civil society, so also many seem to have come to look for the magisterium of the Church to teach economic principles and problems and to instruct and guide them even in matters of a practical and political nature. Nell-Breuning, renowned commentator on the social encyclicals, reminds us of the obvious fact that the Chair of Peter must not be thought of as an academic chair of economics and sociology.[22] The Church, as Pope Pius XI stated in *Quadragesimo anno* (41) does not interpose her authority in technical economic matters, "for which she has neither the equipment nor the mission . . ." She would hardly decide purely prudential matters *ex cathedra*.[23] Prudential decisions in the socioeconomic and political sphere have always been recognized by the Church as being originally and primarily the responsibility of the faithful.

In recognizing and stressing such personal responsibility in concrete decision-making, we are not subscribing to some type of more or less extreme subjectivism or to a denial of the unconditional validity of Catholic social principles. Such basic tenets as the dignity of the human person, the social nature of man, the primacy of the common good, the regulating and constructive function of social justice, the principle of subsidiarity, etc., are, and will remain, inalienable and indefeasible. But we must keep in

22

mind that prudential action concerns means, not ends and as means are conditioned by circumstances. Yet as "virtuous" actions they cannot possibly be unprincipled. They must by their very nature be guided by man's habitual knowledge of the fundamental principles of moral action and follow the bidding of his duly informed conscience. "Therefore," as Josef Pieper has rightly pointed out, "anything that contradicts the natural moral law can never—in no 'concrete situation'—be prudent and good."[24]

The Church's Authority and the Social Apostolate

Yet, all this granted, we must not lose sight of the fact that ecclesiastical authority concerns faith and morals. This authority is not meant to develop specific programs of social action, to propose definite socioeconomic systems, to support political platforms, to submit plans of economic policy, to organize and promote reform movements pursuing practical ends, much less to supply the faithful with more or less detailed "directions for use" in the social apostolate. The Church can never identify herself once and for all with certain devices, formulas, expedients, projects, models, or regimes, though subsidiarily, when extraordinary conditions warrant it, she may do and has done so. In keeping with her indirect powers in temporal matters, the Church has in times of confusion and inaction on the part of the people and their leaders, in emergencies and crises gone far in offering practical advice and direct assistance, in admonishing and urging definite action. In some countries of Latin America, for instance, where Catholics in responsible position have not only failed to take the initiative in establishing social justice, but often failed to see, or deliberately avoided, the issue, the Church has pointed out what she considered needs to be done right then and there. But it is easy to see that this should not have been necessary, just as it should not be necessary for a father to correct and direct his grown children. But do we really need to point to Latin America to demonstrate the failure of Christians to live their faith and the need of the Church to substitute, as it were, for lay initiative? Is it not rather likely that the murderous European resistance movement in Algiers had many Catholics in it? Is it not Catholics who are in the forefront of the anti-integration movement in our own country, in the state of Louisiana? Have the Christians of the West been ready to go all the way in sharing their surpluses with the starving masses in the underdeveloped nations? Could the Father of Christendom be silent where his children fail to speak in word and in deed?

Catholic Social Action

We must not forget, however, as has been pointed out before, that the Church does not speak only through the mouth of the popes. She has, for centuries, spoken through the words and deeds of her bishops, priests, and devoted lay leaders. Yet it has been argued that the Church failed to speak up when Smith's *Wealth of Nations* (1776), Malthus' *Essay on Population* (1789), the *Communist Manifesto* (1848), or Marx' *Das Kapital* (1867 f.) were published. The history of the Catholic social movement gives the lie to such rash and sweeping statements. While the Catholics of the modern world have little reason to rest contentedly on their somewhat meager laurels, they have a right to point with some pride to men like de Mun and de la Tour du Pin of France, C. von Vogelsang and A. M. Weiss, O.P. of Austria, Bishop von Ketteler and Fr. H. Pesch, S.J., of Germany, Cardinal Gibbons and Msgr. John A. Ryan of the United States, Cardinal Manning and Fr. Plater of England, C. Decurtins and Cardinal Mermillod of Switzerland, Périn and Bishop Doutreloux of Belgium, Pastoors and Schaepman of Holland, Soderini and Toniolo of Italy—to name only a few of the many who in various parts of the world at various times have demonstrated the deep and genuine interest of the Church at large in the social question.

Strange as it may seem, it appears necessary to point out the obvious, namely that the Church can hardly be expected to take a stand on a problem before it arises. Yet it has seriously been argued that it took the Church almost nineteen hundred years before she awakened to, and defined her position toward, the social question. The first encyclical to deal with social problems, it is argued, was *Rerum novarum* which appeared in 1891—after everybody else had had his say. It should be obvious that it does not take encyclicals and allocutions to make the Christian principles of social ethics known and binding. Of course, these principles are contained in the Gospel and in the unwritten precepts of the natural moral law. However, it may at times be necessary for the Church to remind the faithful of these principles and to assist them in the "application" of Christian social doctrine to a historically unique set of problems.

Now the "application" of timeless principles to historical situations is not as simple a matter as it is often presented to be. Principles and application belong to two entirely different and separate strata and one cannot be simply reduced to the other. It is not like "applying" a coat or two of paint to an old surface. Man, his conscience, his will, form the connecting link between the two levels: the level of principles and the level of action. It takes a careful study of the situation, which is necessarily singular or unique, to come to what seems to be the right conclusion. Except in matters of justice, which deals with external things and not, as other moral virtues, with interior passions, such conclusions and the subsequent decisions are subject to change.[25] There simply is not one inference, one judgment, and one decision that applies, once and for all, to all persons, all places, and all times. It is an exceedingly doubtful procedure to claim that certain practical conclusions supposedly drawn from the encyclicals or from the writings of St. Thomas are binding in conscience for everyone, everywhere, and at any time. And yet, something like this is done constantly, exhibiting a widespread, profound misconception of the function and purpose of the encyclicals or of "Catholic social principles" in general. Daniel A. O'Connor, C.S.V., a student of the distinguished Flemish sociologist, C. van Gestel, O.P., rightly says that it is "absurd" to expect from the encyclicals "a definite solution immediately applicable to every problem, regardless of where and when it arose."[26]

In their excellent book, The Church and Social Justice, Jean-Yves Calvez, S.J., and Jacques Perrin, S.J. (Chicago: Regnery, 1961), at p. 61, draw attention to the fact that practice and precept interact. They quote Pius XII, who, in a letter of May 8, 1955, to the Third Congress of the International Federation of Christian Workers' Movements, said, "Not only is social doctrine a constant guide for practice, it is itself also guided by practice."

General principles and universal laws are of limited heuristic value in any effort to comprehend qualitatively unique combinations of circumstances. While the philosopher will take what has been called the monothetic approach and stress the common es-

25

sence of varied historical phenomena, the social scientist will apply the so-called idiographic principle and concentrate his attention on the factors which account for the development and determination of their individual differences. Not only the historian, the sociologist, the political scientist, and the economist but also the statesman, the legislator, the administrator—any decision-maker and any person in a position of authority is called upon to unfold and understand the meaning and significance of the peculiar constellation of conditions and events with which he is confronted.[27] One of the hallmarks of leadership is the ability to detect and interpret the nonduplicable, unrenewable elements of a situation as it is one of the distinguishing characteristics of the able historian to be able to fit the pieces of a historical puzzle together until they make "sense," that is until they form a complete and comprehensible picture. For both it is a matter of understanding participation, of empathy, which is probably more an art than a science, the art of hermeneutics, of interpretation, and exposition.

Society and the Social Question

Once this is understood, one can see that there is no ground for the statement that the Church had for nineteen-hundred years failed to see and pass judgment on the social question: for there was no uniform social question throughout the nineteen centuries of Church history, nor was there a repetition of the same or a similar set of problems.

If we want to understand the position of the Church toward the social question of today, we must try to fathom the very uniqueness of that question. If ever there was a social question that involved the social order as such, that is, the ways and manners in which men live and act together, it is that social question which faces us today. In other words, it is not a question that concerns merely the farmers or the townsmen, the slaves or the serfs, the journeymen or the middle classes, nor even merely the laboring men. Basically, it concerns society itself. Here we are confronted with a strange and striking paradox, somewhat perplexing also because of its semantic complications: The modern social question is rooted in the rise of a "society" which is actually a negation of society. Confusion, however, can be avoided if we distinguish

26

carefully between the *historical* phenomenon of society, and the *general* concept of society. If we conceive of society as a stable group of human beings cooperating to achieve some common good, or simply as men in interdependence and interaction, we are forming an ahistorical concept, applicable everywhere and any time. The historical concept of "society," however, has limited validity. Society in this particular sense did not exist before the advent of capitalism, not even in the vocabulary of the learned. It came into existence simultaneously with and as a complement to the (modern) "state," which itself did not exist before that time, not even terminologically.[28] The dichotomy "state and society" is an entirely new phenomenon both in fact and in concept.[29]

What is "Society"?

It cannot be the task of this paper to present an exhaustive study of this phenomenon, even though it is basic to the understanding of the modern social question. We must confine ourselves to sketching the ideal (in a methodological-epistemological sense) type of modern society. It is important to realize from the outset what "society" is *not*: It is not an identifiable group like the folk, the people, the estate, the parish, the guild, the monastic community. In other words, it does not constitute a vital totality but merely a form of social coexistence. It is some kind of informal contractual arrangement between individuals for the pursuit of coincidental and reciprocal, rather than common, interests. Prior to the modern dualism between state and society, man's total social relations tended to be absorbed by or identified with the community to which he "naturally" belonged, or to the political unit to which he owed allegiance. From the time of the reception of the Roman law during the Renaissance there can be observed "an increasing tendency towards the conception of an absolute state on the one hand and a society of independent individuals on the other."[30]

Eventually, social interaction was largely reduced to a system of interhuman relationships designed to satisfy individual wants with a minimum of social control. Scheler speaks of an atrophy of supra-individual goals, "replaced by superficial contractual bonds

27

between individuals." Society, then, is nothing more than "the sum total of the actions of unrelated individuals, each, responsible only to himself."[31] This type of action Max Weber calls "societal action" (as distinguished from communal action), "which is oriented to a rationally motivated adjustment of interests."[32]

A society such as the one here described, namely a society without "socii," i.e., without real "members," without ordered unity, is—to that extent—a society in name only. It is actually the negation of society and, historically, could hardly have arisen before the awakening of the individual. Actually, its historical period of gestation lies somewhere between that postmedieval period of early capitalism, mercantilism, or the commercial revolution, and the rising of the third estate in France in 1789.[33] A century ago, the Swiss political scientist J. K. Bluntschli (1808–81) wrote that the entire concept of modern contractual society "finds its natural foundation in the folkways, mores, and ideas of the third estate." "It is not really the concept of a people but the concept of the third estate," which has become the prototype of Western societal patterns.[34]

From Status to Contract

Now, whether it be called bourgeois, civil, secular, contractual or rational–legal society, it is this pragmatic co-existence, this more or less deliberate social construction, in which individual interests are contractually conjoined for more advantageous results, which may be regarded as the root-cause of the social question of our age.[35] It started with what Sir Henry Maine called the movement "from Status to Contract" and may find its historical consummation and, possibly, solution in what Paul P. Harbrecht, S.J., calls the "paraproprietal society" of tomorrow.[36] Talcott Parsons has shown the contractualizing of life, overlapping widely as it does with the use of money and the wide extension of market relationships, to involve an "enormous extension of the mobility of elements essential to coordinated human action . . ." This mobilization and "transvaluation of all values" (Nietzsche) as well as the rapid social changes that go with it, have had, he says, a disorganizing effect. The recent history of the West, he continues, "has been a period of rapid technological change, industrialization,

28

urbanization, migration of population, occupational mobility, cultural, political and religious change. As a function of sheer rapidity of change which does not allow sufficient time to 'settle down,' the result is widespread insecurity—in the psychological, not only the economic sense—of a large proportion of the population with the well-known consequences of anxiety . . ."[37]

Western society has indeed for many generations been in a state of anxiety, turbulence, and ferment. But there is no stage of history that does not have to accomplish, *nolens volens*, the designs of God. Perhaps much of this agitation represents the distress and also the determination of frustrated social nature to reassert itself, searching for ways and means through which man can identify himself again with a new system of human relationship, possibly one where status rather than contract reigns.

The Genesis of Anomic Society

Some years ago, Frank Tannenbaum, Columbia University historian, in an article that did not get the attention it deserved, gave a brilliant account of the genesis of what Emile Durkheim might have called the "anomic" society.[38] Tannenbaum felt that a careful study of the recent centuries of social conflict which record the sometimes slow and unconscious, and at other times, rapid and violent transition "to a preponderantly middle-class, commercial and industrial commonwealth" should convince anyone, "that there was nothing the older society could have done that would have prevented the newer design from taking shape." All that social policy could have done and often did was to find ways and means for this total metamorphosis to take place "with as little violence and destruction as possible."[39]

Tannenbaum masterfully portrays this metamorphosis as a process of progressive social disintegration, yet at the same time demonstrates that the current was not and could not have been all one way. Nature cannot be suppressed all the time and everywhere. The theoretical consistency of an ideology or a movement is forever counteracted by the logic of nature. There were always activities and institutions which, wittingly or not, interfered with and frustrated the atomization of society. In sweeping away the ideational or folk society of the past which no longer answered the needs of the dawning era of industrialization, history paved the way for a functionally organized society of tomorrow, "with men identified and integrated with their industries in a responsible relationship [and] confined in broad groups, having special rights, privileges and immunities . . ."[40]

In the context of this essay, however, our interest is focused not so much on Tannenbaum's vision of a social reorganization, as on his skillful delineation of the structural changes in the social system which took place in the last half millennium. Vividly he depicts the disruption of the organic groupings of the past, based, as many of them were, on unreflective social cohesion, and how it tore men loose from their familial and communal moorings, throwing them upon their own resources: "The timeless custom of being a member of a community, of belonging to a landed estate, of carrying on one's work in a family or a cottage industry, of being identified with a guild, of having a 'mystery,' in short, of being interlaced within a society as a moral person and having a specific 'status,' wore away more or less rapidly and in varying degrees. Man for the first time in his history was individualized to an extent he had never been previously."[41]

This historian Tannenbaum knows, of course, that there have been "masterless" men before, men, who did not "belong." But through all of past history men ordinarily had experienced their joys and sorrows in common. The new order, if "order" it can be called, set them "free" by setting them adrift. Now, if only he had a source of income, man could, if need be, fend for himself —without family, friends, companions, vocational associates, without the communities that used to shelter and protect him. Tannenbaum frequently speaks of a "loosening of the moorings," to show what the "liberation" of the individual really meant. It was a process of disintegration and atomization resulting in that kind of economic and emotional insecurity which fosters social unrest and provides a fertile soil for revolutionary, sociopathic, and criminal behavior patterns. Complex technological and economic changes were at work to erode the order of traditional status, leaving a social residue "composed of isolated, equal and independent persons, who for the first time became responsible only to themselves and irresponsible for the well-being of anyone—even of their closest relatives."

30

"Liberty" and "Equality"

The story of the rise of the "lonely crowd" (D. Riesman), re-told by Tannenbaum, is too well known to be repeated here. Suffice it to say that the potential proletariat, as Sombart called the social by-product of the disintegration of the medieval order, drifted to, or formed, the growing cities and urban slums. Here men were "free" and "equal"—freed of all emotional support, equal in misery and equal for the competitive struggle. Political theory endowed these individuals, assumed to be their own best judges, with inherent rights and immunities. Economists added to this the notion of a competitive harmony as a result of untrammeled economic relationships between autonomous individuals. It was taken for granted that "society was best in which organized social relations and responsibilities were least" and government would not interfere.[42] "The theoretical justification for individualism seemed to lie in the fact that man was related to the government vertically, each by himself, and to society horizontally not at all."[43] The socialists, seeing the oppression of the propertyless by the propertied, proposed a system which would give to each (!) the full product of his labor and which would culminate in a classless society of emancipated individuals each enjoying his own felicity.[44]

Toward a New Concept of Status

Modern man is beginning to see that the core of the social question does indeed consist in the self-negation of society, and in the lack of that moral identity and psychological unity without which men cannot for long function together. Social and personal insecurity, not only of workers, but of all men included in the modern system described above, is *the* social problem clamoring for a solution. In the long run that solution cannot be accomplished by what the economists call "transfer payments" resulting from a governmental redistribution of income, or from social insurance benefits. "Social security institutions cannot be built on a conflict situation."[45] Maldistribution of income and wealth is not the primary problem. It is, at best, a symptom, not a cause. The heart of the question is not in the sphere of distribution but in the sphere of production; it concerns "man the maker" (G. Vann, O.P.). Many aspects of consumption are by their very nature the

31

concern of the individual only. Not so production. Production is essentially a matter of cooperation.[46] The same process which divorced labor from the ownership of the means of production, separated man from his co-workers, isolated him in the midst of the laboring masses. The separation of man from his job, his tools, and his product is the corollary of the divorce of ownership and control in the modern corporation. Now neither owners nor labor have a "spiritual identification with their source of livelihood," a situation which cannot endure.[47] "Man," says Tannenbaum, "has to belong to something real, purposeful, useful, creative; he must belong to his job, to his industry—or it must belong to him. There is no way of permanently separating the two. What gnaws at the psychological and moral roots of the contemporary world is that most urban people, workers and owners, belong to nothing real, nothing greater than their pecuniary interests."[48] Tannenbaum believes that trade unionism has the historical mission of a "gradual remolding of industrial society on the older pattern of status."[49]

In a very similar vein, Peter F. Drucker expects the industrial enterprise to fulfill the promise of status and to "organize function according to the belief in the Dignity of Man as it is expressed in the responsible participation of citizenship" in the industrial community.[50] Drucker feels that "man must have status and function in his society in order to be a person." He even insists that "the oldest term for status is 'personality,'" just as "the oldest term for function is 'member.'" Together, status and function resolve the polarity or "tension" between person and social order. Only a social order which grants *both* to its members can expect their allegiance.[51] "A society that gives no status must appear as oppressive to the members; it does not give justice—the foundation of commonwealths. A society that fails to give function must appear without pattern, meaning or purpose, hence as irrational, demoniac, unpredictable."[52] Status and society, Drucker feels, represent ideas flowing from the Christian concept of man and his destiny, from the dignity of human nature, which must be recaptured and realized if the West is to survive. But, "in our society," Drucker emphasizes, "social mobility is a prerequisite to proper status." He feels that the phrase, "equal opportunity for everybody," expresses what he considers "a major requirement of adequate status-realization today . . . For status is both what the individual is objectively and what society recognizes in him."[53]

The demand for a functional social order has been the essential concern of all the social encyclicals—not primarily for ethical, but for ontological reasons. Since, according to the old scholastic axiom, action follows being, the Church's first concern is the being and nature of society. Consequently, she stresses the quasi-organic and "functional" aspects of social life, yet she neither proposes the restoration of past historical forms nor submits for realization the model of a supposedly universally "Christian" social order.

The following part will show—without any apologetic intent—a recent charge to be without foundation, viz., that the Church attempts to substitute sententious normative knowledge for the interpretation of existential experience.[54] Essentially she has remained, through the ages, the mediatrix between the Word of God and the historical situation. But while she is aware of her historical mission, she is also conscious of her role as guardian of immutable verities. The historical situation is meaningful only in relation to the eternal Word.[55]

EARLY CAPITALISM AND CATHOLICISM

The Three Stages of Modern Capitalism

Since the modern social question originated and developed with the rise and growth of capitalism, a study of the development of this social question should approach its subject matter synoptically, that is, with an eye on the genesis of modern capitalism. Following Werner Sombart's scheme of the history of Western economic institutions, we shall, as he did, distinguish between three stages of modern capitalism: early, climactic (or full), and late capitalism.[56]

Early capitalism is assumed to have existed from the middle of the fifteenth to the middle of the eighteenth centuries. It was ushered in by the so-called commercial revolution. The period of full (or "high") capitalism, taking place between about 1760 and 1914, is considered to represent the "manhood" of capitalism, unfolding its basic principles in their purest form. It is closely linked with the industrial revolution, at least as far as its origins are concerned. The period in which we live, beginning with World War I, has been called the period of late capitalism. It is charac-

33

06228

LIBRARY
COLBY-SAWYER COLLEGE
NEW LONDON, N.H. 03257

terized by what may be called the managerial or organizational revolution.[57]

The whole development is, in a way, a "dialectical" one, for the first stage is distinguished by its monopolistic features, the second by the opposite, namely competition, and the third by a combination or synthesis of both, monopolistic competition. Recognizing a certain polarity in the evolution of an economic system is not necessarily equivalent to subscribing to economic determinism. It seems legitimate to expect the pendulum of history to swing in the opposite direction once some social philosophy or "creed" has been driven to an extreme. At least this is what has actually happened.

Early capitalism can probably be understood best if we contrast it to or compare it with the preceding economic era, particularly with the period of town economy or of the guilds.

Pre-Capitalism

The medieval period of town economy was characterized by a near-perfect coordination between labor and productive property, domestic and business economy, production and consumption. Perhaps these socioeconomic dyads could be compared to nuclei, each safely enclosed in an organic cell: The producer, such as the master craftsman, ordinarily owned his means of production, that is, his shop and his tools. His apprentices and his assistants, the journeymen, were masters in the making. The master was simultaneously workman and owner, which really meant that he was neither a wage earner nor a "capitalist." His establishment was almost invariably connected with, or part of, his home. Shop and home belonged as much to each other as the tools belonged to the artisan and the artisan to his tools. What was earned in the shop served no other purpose than to decently sustain his family, which usually included the learners and helpers in his shop. Since production was limited to a known clientele, supply was fairly adjusted to demand.

Separating Forces of Capitalism

When the spirit of capitalism penetrated these cells, as it were, it acted as a wedge, gradually separating the nuclei, hitherto in

34

near-perfect harmony. The guilds established a *numerus clausus*, that is, they restricted membership so as to concentrate business in the hands of fewer guild masters. The working community, thus, was split in two: the few who owned the means of production and controlled business and the many who, lacking both the means and the prospects of advancement, offered their services for hire. Similarly the business unit, such as the shop, became divorced from the domestic unit, the home, at least to the degree that gain was no longer limited to the goal of earning a livelihood conformable to one's position in the social hierarchy. With the business unit a separate entity, and no longer serving primarily personal or domestic needs or ends, profit came to assume an autonomous role, being its own end, impersonal and cumulative in character. The cumulative nature of profit is expressed in its tendency to be reinvested so as to expand the business and the latter's profit-earning capacity. The expansion of a firm would be impossible or meaningless were demand to be restricted to traditional, localized, or terminable economic needs. Thus, production had to be divorced from, or rather had to surpass, original customer demand. In other words, it had to be directed toward an anonymous market. Demand itself had to be created, stimulated, expanded.

Early capitalism did not entirely reach this point. But it carried in itself the spirit which urged it on in this general direction.

The Make-up of Economic Systems

What "spirit" played a decisive role in the development of capitalism? Every economic system may be assumed to consist of three constituent elements: a) a certain economic spirit or outlook, namely the sum total of the underlying purposes, motives, and rules of behavior; b) a specific economic order or form, that is, the legal, conventional, and moral norms and standards which govern the economic process; c) finally, the particular technique or technology used, which is to say, the means employed by the economy to reach its goal.[58]

Since it cannot be the task of this essay to give a complete account of the genesis of capitalism, its emphasis will be on the spirit of capitalism which may be assumed to have been the prime factor in its rise and growth. Again, a comparative approach is likely to bring out the decisive characteristics more vividly.

35

The Principle of Sustenance

The socioeconomic order of the precapitalistic, especially medieval, era was, as has been pointed out above, characterized by the principle of a decent livelihood in keeping with one's position in the social hierarchy. We find this idea, that is, of a "sustenance economy," serving to nourish, clothe, and house all members of the community according to their station in life, clearly expressed in the writings of St. Thomas, especially where he discusses the virtue of almsgiving and the vice of avarice.[59] But it was not mere theory. Thomas' treatises, while probably unknown not only to the rank and file but also to most of the rulers and the well-to-do, actually reflected the prevailing practice. To cite some examples: There was the common, that is, land held jointly by the villagers to enable each and all to make a living above the mere subsistence level. Then there was the common field system which called for cooperation among the villagers in cultivating and harvesting their assigned fields. The village community usually assigned to each a hide (plowland), which was a measure of land considered sufficient to support a family. There were the rules of the guilds that restricted its members to an amount of business which, like the hide, would suffice to maintain their families in decent comfort. These and many other devices attest to the fact that medieval man really lived the idea that nobody should acquire or possess more than was in keeping with his status or his calling. The striving for gain was not unknown in precapitalistic times. However, as long as such gain was the equivalent of services rendered and risks taken, its pursuit was considered quite compatible with the principle of a decent livelihood.[60] It is this principle which, in the middle of the second millennium after Christ, gradually gave way to the spirit of capitalism.

The Spirit of Capitalism

According to Sombart, the spirit of capitalism is composed of three elements: the spirit of acquisition, the spirit of competition, and the spirit of rationality. It seems to this writer that while all three are indeed essential components of the spirit of capitalism, they came to the fore in historical succession. The spirit of acquisition, while by no means fully developed in the period of early capitalism, was nevertheless the factor decisive for the development away from the sustenance economy of the past toward the market economy of the future. The spirit of competition does not come really into its own before the start of the period of full or high capitalism. When in the period of late capitalism the spirit of acquisition seems again to recede into the background or to change its nature and function, while decentralized competition gives way to so-called countervailing power, the spirit of economic rationality remains on the scene and seems even intensified. Since we are here trying to gain a bird's-eye view of early capitalism, we will confine our discussion of the spirit of capitalism to a brief review of the spirit of acquisition. This spirit fostered the following propensities among those affected by it: the tendency toward limitless acquisition, the tendency toward unconditional acquisition, the tendency toward ruthless acquisition, and, finally, the tendency toward unconstrained acquisition in which the laws of the jungle are in force.[61] It should be evident that the purpose of a modern business firm, especially a corporation, is not to supply its owners, such as the stockholders, or its management with the means of a decent livelihood. A firm which would limit its returns to that which would satisfy the personal or domestic needs or ends of its owner or owners—needs which, even if they are extravagant, are necessarily limited—would not merely limit its size but jeopardize its very existence. Thus the profits of a capitalistic business enterprise are by their very nature "objectivized" and limited only by business opportunities and the ability of its entrepreneur or management to create and/or utilize such opportunities. Theoretically there are, thus, no limits to business profits under capitalism. Because the goal is infinitely removed and at the same time considered absolute, everything else becomes relative or a means toward this remote yet absolute end. In other words, there are no reservations or rival purposes. Thus the tendency of acquisition has to be unconditional. If conflicting goals or interests are not recognized, acquisition gravitates toward disregard of moral principles or human consideration; or, what amounts to the same, an attempt is made to use such principles and considerations as means to improve upon acquisition. Principles, therefore, are not accepted as having moral binding force but rather as expedients or means of choice, i.e., as resources to be employed if their usefulness is indicated. In other words, the spirit of acquisition calls for a removal of all restrictions, complete freedom from regulations other than those that business imposes upon itself for utilitarian reasons.

At no time in the history of capitalism did all these trends and traits reach full development. As a matter of fact, the stage of early capitalism was characterized by many vestiges of the pre-capitalistic socioeconomic order. Nevertheless, there were, of course, changes significant enough to merit at least a summary examination and, it is true, mainly from the historical, rather than from a systematic, point of view.

Origins of Capitalism

About a century ago, social thinkers and social scientists began to become aware of what might be called the qualitative unique-ness and historical singularity of capitalism.[62] Since then the question has again and again been raised: What are the historical reasons for the rise of capitalism, which factors caused it to come into existence, triggered its emergence, aided its growth? Was it the rapid population growth, the discovery of large deposits of precious metals, the crusades, the Reformation, the Calvinist ethics, the secularization of Renaissance Catholicism, the bour-geois mind, the nonconformism of the Jews and other religious minorities in exile, the humanist spirit of individualism, the *auri sacra fames*? Quite often the commercial revolution is said to have spawned early capitalism. But again we might ask: Was it the transfer of trade routes to the great oceans and the consequent de-velopment of world-wide commerce which broadened man's vistas and disengaged his thinking from the supposedly more confined patterns of the past? Or was it the Renaissance frame of mind which inspired the explorers and adventurers to seek new routes and to discover new worlds? We know that "the continuation of these adventures depended almost wholly on the amount of wealth that they were supposed to bring into the countries that fitted out the exploring fleets."[63] But what caused avarice to be-come widespread and powerful enough to propel merchant fleets, turn arables into sheepwalks, change the religious and vocational fraternities of artisans into oligopolistic combinations, convert bourgeois and noblemen into entrepreneurs? There is really no an-swer to all these questions that would not call forth other questions. We must, thus, content ourselves with the realization that no single cause will provide a satisfactory solution to so complex and perplexing a problem.

The Foster Role of the State

Perhaps the most powerful motive force of early capitalism was the state itself, the very state that had just come to light. In a sense, that economic policy of the territorial and city states which we call mercantilism, "simply extended to the wider area of the state the economic feeling of the town."[64] The goal was still the prosperity of the whole rather than that of the individual: "full employment" even if it meant frustration of technological advancement. But in order to achieve this end, the princes often had to coax, exhort, and goad their subjects into seeking their own advantage, for the princes felt that selfishness can, with skill, as the Mercantilist Bernard Mandeville wrote in 1714, "be turned into public benefits."[65] There was no essential difference in this mercantilist endeavor to have individual acquisitiveness serve the wealth of nations and Adam Smith's belief in a system of natural liberty—except that the classical economist aimed to achieve by competition what the mercantilists hoped to accomplish by bounties and penalties, drawbacks and immunities. Curious as it may seem today, it was difficult enough for the prince to entice the more proficient of his subjects away from their unquestioned acceptance of the principle of sustenance by using bribes and intimidation; the prince would have failed utterly had he preached the gospel of laissez faire. Of course, that gospel was just as foreign to the princes themselves as to their subjects; and the same was true of the idea of promoting business for business' sake. And yet the raison d'état accomplished—in a manner reminiscent of Wundt's heterogeneity of purposes—what it did not originally intend to accomplish, namely: it cultivated in the people a taste for profit. And yet, though they began to relish it, they were far from conceiving of gain as something one could ever pursue entirely apart from personal ends and needs. They were, it is true, quite ready to make money—but more in the sense in which St. Thomas thought of money, namely as something the use of which "consists in parting with, spending it."[66] Some enjoyed the role of benefactors and patrons of the arts and sciences, while others relished the comforts of early retirement.

The Role of Mercantilism

It is interesting that the mercantilist governments themselves laid greater stress on the circulation of money within the state than on its accumulation.[67] With all their oddities, the mercantilists were too clever to store treasure simply in order to enjoy the looks of it. After they had broken away from the Holy Roman Empire, the town-territories, the territorial principalities, and eventually the national states, needed money to build up and sustain a standing army of mercenaries to defend their contested and precarious sovereignty. The conspicuous consumption and prodigality of the courts perhaps served as a means of self-reassurance for the secessionist princes, and of demonstrating their independence. Whatever the reason, outfitting soldiers and running castles means putting money into the hands of the people. There it may evoke an increase in consumer demand—without a corresponding increase in investment expenditures. Mercantilism, which had greatly contributed to the rise of secular society, particularly by creating the national state, which in turn opened the door to nationwide marketing, does not seem to have been particularly successful in stimulating capital formation or, more particularly, capital investment. One has to keep in mind that, after all, the princes did not promote manufacture and trade for the sake of merchants, mine-operators and mill-owners; they wanted to raise the tax-paying ability of their subjects rather than the latter's ability to create surpluses for reinvestment. Hence, what great fortunes there were in the age of early capitalism were rarely made in the ordinary course of business activity but more likely by political means, through privileges, purchase of government positions, farming of taxes, usury, looting of colonial areas, and exploitation of colonial peoples.[68] And fortunes of this type were often used for undertakings similar to those from which they had been derived in the first place, rather than invested in regular business enterprises. This is not to deny that funds were available for capitalistic ventures, especially funds derived from the accumulated profits of big merchants and bankers as well as from the considerable rents and profits collected by those of the gentry

40

whose land was now used for urban settlement and industrial purposes.[69] But these funds were small by comparison with the opportunities. Whenever property in kind was converted into moneyed property which could be invested, it was liable to arouse the attention of the prince of the territory. He, like any typical mercantilist statesman, probably had plans for its use that differed from those of the owner. In view of this insecurity many a prospective investor may have preferred to spend and consume what he could not convert into profit-bearing capital of his own choice. While the sustenance idea was still alive, the profit motive did make progress, as did, though to a lesser extent, the technology of production. But where capital formation is slow, not even the most intense spirit of acquisition can accelerate the development of capitalism.

The Church and Emerging Capitalism

It should be evident by now that early capitalism was a period of transition, of adjustment, and of uncertainty. Interhuman relations were still largely of the face-to-face kind and the quest for profit had not as yet become a self-feeding process. It was a historical process that resembled a metamorphosis. Capitalism was struggling out of its cocoon, as it were. Some of the changes that had taken place were striking, others were hidden or undeveloped. With the population growing rapidly, traditional economic forms and methods proved unable to cope with the task of supplying the needs of the people. The business firm and the entrepreneur emerged and with them the concepts and reality of capital and profit. What was the Church's position to the new economic order in the making? As far as this order represented just another economic technique—the use of money and credit, a market economy, economic decision-making by entrepreneurs—she took no stand. It is not her mission to do so. But the role of man in the new order, the position of profit in the hierarchy of values, the means–end relationship in the economic process had and will always have her deep concern.

There is no denying that the economic practice of the Roman Curia from the thirteenth century onward acted as an accelerator for the development of capitalistic banking and the modern credit economy.[70] But it is equally true that the Church was genuinely concerned about the changes that were taking place all around her in the economy and in society. Though the popes did not always practice what they preached, Heilbroner is right in saying that even what disreputable activity there was, "was undertaken despite, and not because of the Church's deepest convictions."[71] Behind the ecclesiastical censure of usury, overreaching, and the unbridled quest for profit, was a firm belief in a hierarchy of values and the relativity of all temporal endeavors and worldly ends. And worldly ends were now pushing upward in the axiological hierarchy. Confusion and uncertainty began to beset the more conscientious of the faithful. The fathers-confessor were confronted with new problems: Is it permissible to provide for an income which would exceed that which is needed for a decent livelihood? Is it lawful for the seller to make an extra charge if the good in question is worth more to him than to the average buyer or seller? Is the price to be determined by supply and demand or by the cost of production? Does the innovative, risk-taking activity (*industria*) of the up and coming entrepreneur entitle him to a special return? Is it legitimate to take advantage of price fluctuations? And so on. It is not unlikely that the parish priests turned to their bishops for advice and that the bishops commissioned their best moral philosophers to investigate and to report about their findings.

Late Scholastics and the New Economy

The writings of St. Antonine of Florence (1389–1459), of Cardinal Cajetan, O.P. (1469–1534), of St. Bernardine of Siena (1380–1444) were attempts to bring moral doctrine "up to date" with the new economic developments. If one reads their treatises and similar ones by Suárez, Duns Scotus, Dominic Soto, Molina, and many others, carefully and without preconceived notions, one cannot possibly hold that their views differed in any *essential* points from those of St. Thomas Aquinas and other medieval scholastics. There is nothing in the writings of Thomas to support the idea that he ever thought of the just price as one fixed once and for all, or that he looked upon it as a static norm. But the economic life of his time was largely static just as that of Antonine and Bernardine had become dynamic. The dynamic nature of the new economic order was not, as such, a moral, much less a dogmatic, issue. It was largely a datum just as the mechanization of production some 350 years later was such a fact to be reckoned with. Thus it was quite natural and even necessary for the moral philosophers of the Renaissance to take into account the dynamic market changes as price-determining factors, to deal with credit purchases and sales, with the wage of the then slowly rising class of propertyless laborers. Here we have an instructive example of the relationship between principle and fact-situation discussed in the first part of this essay. The theologian as theologian was and is not concerned with cultural, technical, organizational, or political changes as such, but only insofar as they bear on faith and morals. Buying and selling on credit, for instance, was a relatively new technique in the equally new field of marketing. The moralist's question was: "Is it compatible with justice, with the doctrine of usury, to charge a higher price in case of deferred payment?" Obviously, an agreement to "buy now and pay later" is not intrinsically wrong. In view of the subjective and thus changeable elements and the uncertainty of human valuation in the process of price determination, Antonine, the Dominican, and Bernardine, the Franciscan, distinguished between three levels of the just price. The upper limit (rigidus) would apply to purchases on credit, the medium (discretus), to cash sales, and the lower (pius), to cases where the merchant wished to do a favor.

Profits and Interest

More interesting is the fact that the two mendicant friars were fully aware of the function of capital. Their orders were typically urban products and residing, as they did, in Italy's most important trading cities, they had all the experiences of a commercial environment. Bernardine formally recognized the gain-creating function of original investment and called the money used in commercial enterprises "capital."[72] Antonine also distinguished between investment (ratio capitalis) and moneylending (mutuum), denying the productivity of coin, but admitting that of "capital," as an instrumental cause.[73] However, since it is productive only in the hands of the businessman, the entrepreneur, not of itself, there seems to be no essential difference between money on the one hand, and the technical means of production (instrumenta) as well as funds designated for investment on the other. Man re-

43

mains the principal efficient cause of the returns from capital. The question may be raised whether Antonine, in stressing the importance of capital as an indispensable means in the creation of utilities and the pursuing of a business, did not demonstrate property as such to be a legitimate source of income. Obviously, not only would capital be unproductive without human effort (*industria*), human effort would be of little avail without the use of capital. In any case, Antonine by supporting Thomas' theory of private property at least implicitly proved that the owner is entitled to that share of the total business income which can be imputed to his investment or to an amount fair and yet sufficient to make investment worth his while. Obviously in a partnership (*societas*) as in a corporation even the managerially inactive member who provided "only" the capital, or part of it, has a right to a share in the total business returns. Antonine's theory of profit would be quite pointless if such profit would be just another name for wages or wages of management. Actually, in his own *Summa* (III, 4, 8 and III, 8, 3) he is quite explicit in justifying the enterpriser's income.[74] In this connection it is interesting to see that Bernardine prefers "a man to enrich himself in order to profit his neighbor by new enterprises, rather than to sit idle for fear of growing too rich."[75]

Free Trade vs. Restraint of Trade

Antonine, who was known for his extraordinary concern for the underprivileged and for his active charity, and Bernardine, who made a name for himself as a very strict reformer of his order and a powerful penitential preacher, both championed the cause of the merchant. He was not to be looked upon as a necessary evil whose activities, while not necessarily sinful, can hardly if ever be pleasing to God. This does not prevent either of them from listing and criticizing severely the numerous abuses then current among merchants, particularly their attempts to restrain trade. Like Adam Smith some 300 years later, Antonine frowns upon and castigates all form of collusion, corners, speculative business combines, in short, all monopolistic and oligopolistic practices serving private advantage. He is opposed to combinations and the authorizing of monopolies because their purpose is the artificial securing of dearer prices. He and most of the late scholastic moral philosophers seem convinced that the market price, freely arrived at, is more likely to be just than any "fixed" price. Naturally, during the Middle Ages, when exchange was as a rule interpersonal or between non-competing groups, when a full-fledged, impersonal, competitive market did not, as yet, exist, the emphasis of moral doctrine was on the objective elements of cost. With the widening of the exchange relations, emphasis began to shift toward supply and demand as price–determining agents. The price was likely to be fair, it was pointed out, if it was the result of a truly free agreement between buyers and sellers, if it was the currently accepted price, if it was in accordance with the common estimate, if it put neither the supplier nor the purchaser at a disadvantage. Since the supply was assumed to represent the cost of production, the late scholastic writers seem to have taken it for granted that in the long run no seller could agree to a price which did not cover his expenses. This would be entirely in keeping with the undisputed proposition of modern economics that under conditions of free competition prices tend to equal costs of production, including normal "profits."

The Church and the Entrepreneurial Economy

It should be evident that these views of late scholastic writers regarding the justice of price were not alarmingly novel. Neither did they, as Edgar Salin asserts, open the gates of the Church to the emerging credit economy.[76] Nor did the Church or her recognized teachers have any intention of either overthrowing the old or of introducing a new socioeconomic order. This was not their mission. But the Church was and will always be concerned about justice and charity in any order, new or old. Making profit an end in itself was and is incompatible with her teachings. But she was not opposed to "an economic system characterized by private property, by production for a market and by the phenomenon of credit."[77] As a matter of fact, in the encyclical, *Vix pervenit*, of November 1, 1745, Benedict XIV pointed out that the Church did not consider the institution of investment credit and the return from capital as violating justice.[78] But the Church never really revised her teachings on usury: In the case of a contract of mutuum, i.e., of a loan of money (or other fungible goods), also called a loan for consumption, there is never a justifiable reason for exacting a premium. Even the so-called extrinsic reasons[79] do

45

not entitle the lender to a gain from the loan as such; they merely justify a compensation for a deprivation of some sort so as to restore the equilibrium of commutative justice. But with the rise of capitalism the contract of *mutuum* (the consumptive loan) became relatively unimportant while the investment loan, business partnership, and, eventually (the acquisition of) corporate stock developed into strong institutional supports of the up and coming economic system.[80] Without profitable capital investment, this system could not possibly have served the objective purpose (*finis operis*) of any economic system, namely the satisfaction of the physical needs of society. Long before the advent of capitalism the Church recognized as just a claim for "gain" as a compensation for *periculum* (perils, risk) and for *industria* (entrepreneurship, innovative activity). A man who joined a partnership (*societas, contractus trinus*) was considered entitled to a share (dividend) in the profits of the firm because he exposed himself to the risk of loss (of *his* funds, because the partner is not a creditor!). A person who had an opportunity to invest his money in a profitable enterprise of this kind, but lent it instead to someone else, could, under the title of *lucrum cessans* claim an indemnification (*interesse*, not *usura!*), from the borrower, equivalent to the certain or at least very probable gain he had foregone.[81] Sombart suspects that the ecclesiastical prohibition of interest (usury) and the Church's approbation of capital gain contributed to the advancement of capitalism since men of means, instead of lending money at interest, would invest it in profitable (though risky) enterprises.[82] Be that as it may, there can be no doubt that the Church never questioned the justice of interest in the sense economists use the term today, namely as a return for the use of funds spent for capital equipment.

The Concept of Status

In the period of early capitalism even the principle of a decent livelihood in keeping with one's status was, it seems, no longer considered a definite barrier to increasing income. Cardinal Cajetan, commenting on Thomas' supposedly static concept of man's station in society, which seemed to say that a *rusticus* should always remain a *rusticus* (peasant), an *artifex* always an *artifex* (artisan), a *civis* always a *civis* (subject? freeman?), exclaimed

"quae sunt manifeste absurda" ("which is obviously absurd").[83]
This is not to say that the idea of an income in accord with one's
calling and status was abandoned; what was abandoned—if it was
ever held (cf. supra, note 60)—was the notion that nobody should
ever try to rise above his station, a notion which would fix every
person's income and property for the whole span of his life. But a
rise in the social hierarchy was, it seems, generally thought of as
justifiable only on the basis of one's qualification as a member of
the social body—an idea definitely opposed to the notion of
privileges and oligopoly typical for early capitalism though not
entirely foreign to the manorial and guild eras of the Middle
Ages.[84]

Christian Humanism and Human Dignity

The greater appreciation of the individual person, that was
typical of the age of humanism, also found expression in a greater
regard for the lower classes of rural society, the serfs and the small
peasants, as well as the slaves. We know that already during the
Middle Ages the usurer, the extortioner of the poor, was severely
punished by the Church. The Church has really never, up to this
day, changed her teaching that a person's superfluity, i.e., that
which exceeds the needs of his station, belongs to the poor. She has
always taught that in times of extreme necessity those in need
have a claim of right to all that exceeds a person's minimum of
subsistence, provided the poor need it to survive. The more individualistic interpretation of the concept of private property crept
into the teachings of moral philosophers only in the eighteenth
and nineteenth centuries.[85] During the time of the enclosures in
England, the Church's saintly humanist, Thomas More, used
the vehicle of a travel book to bring to the attention of his contemporaries the sufferings of the English peasantry and the horrible
injustices inflicted upon those who had been ejected from field
and home by their greedy lords.[86] The story of the "Christian"
lords and merchants of the age of the Renaissance is often anything but edifying. Today the West is reaping the whirlwind of
the colonial policies of Christian rulers and merchants in the age
of the discoveries and explorations. Alongside with the most
shameless predatory exploitation of the natural resources of colonial peoples there took place the even more outrageous exploita-

47

tion of their human resources, often to the utter confusion of the missionaries who had gone to these regions to preach the gospel of love and the precepts of justice. It is understandable that in the eschatological climate of the early Church the emphasis of Christian writers dealing with the problem of the *servus* was on the slavery of sin and the origin of slavery in the fall of man,[87] but it is hard to understand why even so open-minded a man as Antonine could devote many pages of his *Summa moralis* to a discussion of the rights of slaveholders and the duties of slaves as if it was an institution never even to be questioned from a Christian point of view.[88] The slave traders of the sixteenth and following centuries may well have taken comfort from these treatises even though they were certainly never meant to vindicate and defend the inhumanities perpetrated by the man hunters and slave traders of the colonial age. St. Thomas considered slavery an institution not based on nature but on the common law of nations (*jus gentium*) and yet while considering it an institution merely of *relative* natural law, he did not think that some sort of servitude could ever be wholly abolished. It is gratifying, then, to hear of the profound indignation of Queen Isabella when Columbus, in order to cover up the ill success of his second expedition, sent her a shipload of slaves. She wanted to see the Indians converted to the faith of Christ rather than enslaved.[89] Francis J. Gilligan, one of the foremost American pioneers for interracial justice, states that while it must be admitted that the trading of African Negroes had its origin and earliest development among a people who were professedly Catholic, the Portuguese and the Spaniards, it is "equally true that these peoples cooperated in that trade in direct violation of the prohibitions of the leaders in their Church, the Popes." "As early as October 7, 1482," Msgr. Gilligan reports, "at the time of the exploration of the western coast of Africa, Pope Pius II vehemently censured the Portuguese who dared to sell into bondage men like themselves. After the discovery of the new world, Paul III declared it was an invention of the devil to affirm that Indians may be reduced to servitude. The same prohibitions were repeated on April 22, 1639 by Urban VIII, and in the year 1741 by Benedict XIV. Pope Gregory XVI in 1839 only summarized the constant teaching of his predecessors when he wrote 'we earnestly warn and admonish in the Lord all Christians of whatever condition they may be and enjoin on them that no one

48

shall dare in the future unjustly to annoy Indians, Negroes and other men—or to exercise this inhuman traffic.' "[90]

But after the time of the Reformation the power and influence of the Church in worldly matters declined rapidly and few of the secular authorities would now listen to the voice from Rome.

FULL CAPITALISM AND CATHOLICISM

The Rise of Full Capitalism

During the middle of the eighteenth century, considerable changes began to take place both in the structure of economic society and in the mentality of the peoples of the West. Again we are confronted with the question: What were the propelling forces of these changes? As always in history, they were of a factual and an ideological nature. The topic of this essay directs our interest especially toward the latter.

Men had been living for some three centuries under various forms of absolutism, benevolent or otherwise. Paradoxically, it was from their potentates and overlords that they had also learned how to make money and how, in a way, to stand on their own feet. Now they began to grow tired of regimentation and regulations. Even some of the governments had become weary of stringing red tape and supervising the citizens and their activities. Perhaps they were, at long last, realizing that their regulations, tariffs, and decrees discouraged initiative and self-responsibility to the detriment of the polity. At any rate, the spirit of liberty and independence began to stir in many places.

Mercantilist Origins of Laissez Faire

It is important to realize, however, that the very same mercantilism which we know to have seriously crippled many industries through its system of regulations and restrictions, carried in itself some of the seeds of the economic liberalism of the age of full capitalism. As the Swedish economist Eli F. Heckscher has pointed out, mercantilism implied a general view of society closely akin to that of the laissez faire philosophers. "Both followed the general trend of modern opinion, replacing religious and moral considera-

49

tions by belief in unalterable laws of social causation—a rationalism often accompanied by a strictly non-moral and non-humanitarian view of social life."[91] Heckscher draws attention to the fact that J. B. Colbert, French mercantilist statesman (whose system of planned controls caused French mercantilism to be called "Colbertism"), favored noninterference and free trade. Supposedly, his edicts and *règlements* were meant to remove the causes of all restraints of trade—like "the war to end all wars." At any rate, it is significant that an English mercantilist, John Hales—two hundred years before Smith's *Wealth of Nations*—explained the mechanics of the price system and expressed his belief that the power of self-interest would effect the most efficient allocation of resources.[92] Nevertheless, it was Colbert's governmental guidance and assistance of industry, which caused J. C. Gourney, a prephysiocratic merchant and himself a government official, to coin the phrase, *laissez faire*. The essence of physiocracy is indeed not merely a protest against the undervaluation of agriculture by mercantilists but also, and not least of all, a belief in the "natural" foundation of economic life. It is the natural laws of economy which according to the physiocrats "illumine man's conscience" and in this manner "reduce the need for legislation."[93]

"Revolutionary" Origins of Full Capitalism; The American Revolution

It has been suggested that the Enlightenment and the complex of eighteenth-century revolutions meant for full capitalism what the Renaissance and Reformation had meant for early capitalism. The influence of deism, the "religious" variety of Enlightenment, upon classical economics has been established beyond doubt. Adam Smith's notion of the "invisible hand" of providence which directs the economic process was deism pure and simple.[94] But what about the revolutions? It goes without saying that the American Revolution was a revolt against British mercantilism or mercantilist colonialism. But it was more than that. As A. M. Simons put it, it was part of a world-wide violent upheaval of society by which the up-and-coming "capitalist" overthrew feudalism and came into power. As far as the North American colonies were concerned, it was to some extent a conflict between the Whigs and the Tories on both sides of the Atlantic—the Whigs representing a still new and undeveloped kind of competitive capitalism, the Tories representing the feudal lords joined by the old protectionist merchant class. Simons felt that the dominant interests in the revolutionary party were the same which elsewhere and at other times were emphasized by capitalist businessmen. He also expressed the opinion that in the days of the Revolutionary War, employers, wage earners, and farmers alike were imbued with the capitalist mind.[95] At any rate, it is certainly more than a coincidence that it was in 1776, the year of the Declaration of Independence that Adam Smith published his *Wealth of Nations*, which has been acclaimed as "the most cogent and most famous attack on Mercantilism ever written."[96] The same idea which animated the *Wealth of Nations*, the idea of natural liberty, also inspired the Declaration of Independence.

Economic Implications of the French Revolution

The sparks of the new concept of economic and political freedom soon leaped from America to France. It is a known fact that the Frenchmen who drew up the *Déclaration des droits de l'homme et du citoyen* were well acquainted with the constitutions of the new American states and the bills of rights embodied in them. This gives credence to Jellinek's proposition that the idea of human rights, which the Puritans had carried to New England, had returned again to Europe and had sparked the French Revolution.[97] But we must not overlook the possibility that the general economic *malaise*, the decline of the prices for wine and grain, as well as crop failures, droughts, unemployment, and the like eased the way for the French Revolution. It is significant, however, that while the revolution abolished feudalism, it did not abolish the institution of private property. After all, this was a bourgeois—not a proletarian—revolution, even though the bourgeoisie did not mind having the small peasants and the urban poor fight its battles. Certainly, church lands and the landed property of the crown and of the political emigrants were confiscated. But when the government, in order to obtain revenue, sold these estates by auction, it was the men with money: the bourgeoisie, country lawyers, and newly-rich merchants who acquired them. The peasants could not even get the revolutionary legislatures to protect their grazing rights because these "privileges" were regarded as

51

relics of a barbarous past and incompatible with individual freedom. The bourgeois concept of freedom was demonstrated in the abolition of the usury laws, the suppression of the guilds, and the right given to landed proprietors to work their land any way they pleased. The revolution did, it is true, remove the privileges of the estates and proclaimed equality before the law, but those social conditions which rested on differences in wealth and income remained. The LeChapelier Law of 1791, supposedly meant to prevent the return of vocational corporations, thereby safeguarding the democratic process, actually blocked the formation of any labor organization, that is, of combinations that might have questioned the prevailing distribution of property. Again, it was in the name of liberty that the syndicates or unions were forbidden. The revolution, thus, which had done little for the peasants, did yet less for the workers—though both belonged to the third estate. But it did create a *new* bourgeoisie which used the spoils of the revolution to lay the groundwork for the industrial capitalism soon to come.

The Agrarian Revolution

A French historian, Leopold V. Deslisle, in his studies of agriculture and farm labor in Normandy in the Middle Ages (1851) wrote that a thirteenth-century peasant would have felt quite at home on many peasant holdings in the France of the mid-nineteenth century. Not so in England, for there was at the very same time a veritable agrarian revolution in the making. Of course, in England the enclosure movement between the fifteenth and the seventeenth centuries had already changed the rural picture to a striking degree. But in the eighteenth and in the beginning of the nineteenth centuries, the enclosure movement was speeded up and intensified to a degree that represented something really new and revolutionary. Even though this process depopulated the countryside and rapidly increased the numbers of the potential proletariat, writers now praised the enclosures as a necessary condition of economic progress. It cannot be our task to describe in detail the changes which made large-scale farming profitable. We must content ourselves to note that "pressure was exerted upon agriculture to give up its traditional methods and time–honored system of land tenure and to enter into the path of capitalism."[98]

The Industrial Revolution

The agricultural revolution may be said to have partly preceded and laid the foundation for an industrial revolution. Lacking the expropriated and displaced farmers, ready to work for daily wages in the manufacturing plants and the factories slowly arising, capitalism would have lacked the manpower without which capital would have remained sterile. Much of the industrial raw material was still organic in nature and thus came from the countryside. This was particularly true of sheep's wool, flax, hemp, and hides. In the eighteenth century there developed two serious bottlenecks to industrial production. First, progressive deforestation caused a shrinkage of the wood supply needed for construction, cabinet making, and fuel. Secondly, hand spinning was no longer able to meet the rapidly-increasing demand for yarn. Small wonder, then, that inventors concerned themselves primarily with the problems of inorganic fuels and mechanized spinning. Since the beginning of the seventeenth century, English experiments had used mineral coal instead of charcoal for the smelting of iron ore, but it was not before 1740 that the first blast furnace was fired with coke. However, large-scale production of iron in coke furnaces awaited James Watt's perfection of the steam engine so it could be used to pump water from mine shafts, force blasts of air through molten iron and drive heavy iron rolling machines.[99] It is an interesting "coincidence" that the first satisfactory steam engine was completed by Watt in 1776, the year, as will be remembered, of the Declaration of Independence and of the publication of the first edition of Smith's *Wealth of Nations*. And it was in 1776 when John Wilkinson's steam blast, obtained from a Watt engine, brought the coking process to perfection.[100] It should be mentioned at least in passing that while a professor at Glasgow University, Adam Smith had become acquainted with James Watt, a young instrument maker who had been expelled from the city proper by the guild and had been given haven by the university. The two bachelors became intimate friends, and later startled the world, one with his philosophy of competition, the other with his application of physical science to industrial technology.[101]

In the 1760s the Society of Arts and Manufacturers offered prizes for a workable and efficient spinning machine. Hargreaves' famous "Spinning Jenny," invented about 1767, allowed one spinner to spin simultaneously eight, then sixteen, and eventually more than a hundred threads of yarn, and was so simple and inexpensive that it did not change the homework nature of the spinning industry. But with Arkwright's invention of a spinning frame driven by water, and Crompton's invention of a "mule" for simultaneously drawing and twisting fiber into yarn and winding it on spools, the machinery became too large and heavy for the spinner's home. It could be used only where power—first wind or water, later steam—was available. This ended (about 1788) the domestic system of spinning. Now the yarn supply was adequate, but there were not enough weavers. Kay's flying shuttle, which in 1733 had roused the weavers' wrath, was in 1785 embodied in Edmund Cartwright's power loom. A crude device, it nevertheless opened the way for the eventual mechanization of the entire textile industry.

The Triad of Science, Engineering, and Business

Particularly interesting is the fact that now not only was science applied to engineering problems, but engineering was also called upon to assist in business projects. The partnership of James Watt with Matthew Boulton, a Birmingham manufacturer of novelties, concluded in 1779, brought about a union between a captain of industry and a scientifically-trained engineer, and may indeed be looked upon as symbol of a new alliance.[102] Arkwright's partnership with two wealthy hosiers, Need and Strutt, was another symbol of the fact that engineering and manufacturing were subordinated to business and to the merchant almost from the beginning of the industrial revolution. This should not be surprising, in view of the early need for capital which mechanics and inventors rarely could supply.

The Rise of the Industrial Proletariat

But with the rise of the factory system, still another dependency came into focus: that of the propertyless wage earner upon his employer. Even during the period of early capitalism it was still rather generally acknowledged that "To every class and every individual God has assigned his sustenance."[103] Now, however, people asked themselves seriously what they could do to keep the poor poor so that they would always be ready to work, and to do so for low wages. Robert Heilbroner quotes "a leading moralist" who in 1723 is supposed to have written: "To make society happy, it is necessary that great numbers should be wretched as well as poor."[104] Yet, while some seem to have been convinced that it was God's will that the poor were poor (especially since their poverty was supposedly essential to the wealth of the nation), there were others who recognized pauperism as an evil and who "could not see how poverty could create wealth."[105] Even if Arnold Toynbee's suggestion that industrialization had reduced the English factory worker "to an Asiatic standard," cannot be verified historically, and even if Friedrich Engels' description of the *Condition of the Working Class in England* (1845) represents a gross exaggeration, the actual record is bad enough. [106] As early as 1797 the English economist Eden speaks of the "labouring poor . . . whose daily labor is necessary for their daily support,"[107] thus unwittingly defining the modern proletariat. Perhaps, in those days it was even a subproletariat, because their daily labor did *not* by far earn them their daily support. Many, if not most, laborers had to send their wives and children to the factories and mines to have them help him eke out a meager living. The intimate, face-to-face contacts which had characterized the relationship between the master and his fellow workers in the craft shop and in the manufacturing plant gave way to a "cash nexus." The polarization of society into antagonistic classes, a process which had been going on ever since the advent of capitalism, now gained momentum. Eventually, society did seem to be "composed of a mass of anonymous, rootless individuals with little in the way of intimate ties to their fellow men."[108] Whatever the degree of actual depersonalization of interhuman relations—nature can never be expelled "for good"—the end of the eighteenth and the beginning of the nineteenth century undoubtedly witnessed the birth of class society. And with it the birth of the modern "social question." Significantly, the sociologists and political scientists who discovered and analyzed the contractual, segmental, secular, or "secondary" group society, were among the first to recognize and identify its class character and the rise of an urban proletariat: Lorenz von Stein, Robert von Mohl, but also Louis Blanc, Saint-Simon, Hegel, and Catholics like Adam Müller, Franz von Baader, Joseph M. von Radowitz—practically all of them long before Karl Marx.[109]

The Idea of Competition

The industrial revolution was in the first place a movement which brought technological innovations such as power-driven machinery and more efficient methods of iron and steel production. It would, thus, be folly to make it responsible for the rise of the proletariat and all the miseries inflicted upon it. Yet, as G. P. McEntee has rightly pointed out, it was unfortunate for the working class that "this stupendous revolution, synchronized with the prevalence of a spirit of individualism which, permeating every department of thought and activity, brought about a philosophy of laissez-faire in matters social and economic."[110] Free competition, which during the mercantilist stage of Capitalism was under a certain disparagement, became the central idea and moving force of economic life. Of course, theorizing about, and the rationalization of, competition lagged behind the changes and practices which theory, especially economic theory, was trying to interpret.[111] Before business could engage in full-fledged competition, it had to rid itself of the last shackles of mercantilism and embrace the idea that the purpose of business enterprise is the pursuance of its own self-interest. No theory is needed to convince business that in the long run a firm, especially if it is one of many of its kind, cannot ordinarily serve its own interest if it does not at the same time serve the interest of its customers and thus secure their favor. This can, as a rule, be achieved by offering customers terms more favorable than those offered by other firms through the improvement of quality and/or the reduction of prices. Reduction of prices, on the other hand, normally calls for a reduction of the cost of production; and this requirement, in turn, stimulates inventions that help increase efficiency and productivity. Whether new methods and new instruments of production, increased efficiency and output really "pay" depends, of course, as Adam Smith pointed out, on the extent and, we might add, on the behavior and responsiveness, of the market. The extent, behavior, and responsiveness of the market, however, are not merely accepted as immutable data. One of the main functions of the modern entrepreneur is "innovation," that is, the changing of these data, so as to make them serve the maximization of income. Advertising, stimulating new demands, finding new outlets for products, opening up of new markets, and so on, are, together with cost reduction, part and parcel of such innovating activity.[112]

The Monetization and Mobilization of Life

Robert H. Heilbroner has shown that the transition from the precapitalistic era of tradition and the early capitalistic epoch of command to the full capitalistic period of market transactions presupposes the monetization of the factors of production. By monetization he means the putting of a price tag on everything: everything now is "for sale," as it were. Price directs the allocation of scarce resources. The dollar bill becomes the admission ticket to these short supplies. Money is the open-sesame, except that there is nothing magical about it. Like Sombart, Talcott Parsons, Tawney, and others, Heilbroner stresses the mobilization of life in the age of full capitalism, not only in the traditional sense of social, spatial, occupational, and class mobility, but also in the sense of a mobilization of the factors of production, especially of capital and labor, but, paradoxically, also of "immovables" (realty).[113]

Praedial bondage, by which a peasant was forever attached to the soil, to a piece of land, had all but disappeared. Entail and primogeniture, by which lands were inalienably bestowed upon a certain person or certain persons, were rapidly abolished in the industrializing countries. This was in line with the progressive depersonalization of the relation between producer and consumer. Buyer and seller, as a rule, no longer haggled about a commodity. The price was set and the customer might take it or leave it. All merchandise tended to become standardized so that personal bargaining on the basis of differences in the quality or quantity of such merchandise would be without object and to no purpose. Standardized merchandise presupposes simplified, stereotyped, and, wherever and whenever possible, mechanized production, reducing considerably the need for skilled workmen and thus permitting standard labor contracts. To the depersonalization and commercialization of labor relations there corresponds the "objectification" of credit relations through the use of negotiable, marketable securities, transferable by indorsement and/or delivery irrespective of the persons involved.

57

Capitalist Dynamics and Human Insecurity

The separation of the producer—taking the term in its widest sense—from the means of production, the divorce of the income-earning unit, such as the shop, from the domestic economy, and the disjunction of production and consumption create a somewhat artificial situation which tends to engender a sense of uncertainty and insecurity. Even a high standard of living cannot quite remove the awareness of one's dependence on market-chances, that is, on the opportunities of business for profitable sales, and on the turn of the market, the business cycle. Capitalism, after all, is essentially dynamic, that is, an economic system characterized by entrepreneurial innovations, free consumer choice, and a high degree of human interdependence. All this makes for insecurity—which is the price of freedom. The social costs of the private enterprise system, which fall upon the community, are high. Consumer choice is fickle and faddish, constantly endangering investments. Innovations too may destroy and wipe out jobs in one place while creating new investment and employment opportunities in another. Progressive specialization and labor-saving mechanization tend to render the individual worker expendable or at least replaceable. Wage determination is not primarily a matter of equivalence and of earning a livelihood, but one of cost of production and of bargaining power. As far as breadwinning is concerned, the father is usually no longer in a position of unquestioned superiority. His wife and his adult children are likely to be his peers in the shop and in the business of making a living. Thus, along with the hierarchical patterns of the past, the family also tends to disintegrate and, in disintegrating, to accelerate the transformation of the primary and ideational or status society into the secular and contractual society discussed above.

Commercialism and Christianity

With this sketch of full or high capitalism completed, we are now ready to ask the question about the role of Catholicism in general and of the Church in particular within this historical setting. Max Weber once expressed the opinion that the thoroughly monetary and therefore impersonal and abstract nature of the capitalist market economy makes that economic system almost impervious to ethical reflections and scrutiny. Paternalistic relations such as existed between the patron and his manumitted slaves, the paterfamilias and his servants, the manorial lord and his serfs, the master craftsman and his journeymen and apprentices, and the other than the purely commercial relations which capitalism created in the labor market, were of a personal human character and therefore could be "developed and penetrated ethically."[114] "But it is not possible to regulate—at least not in the same sense or with the same success—the relations between the shifting holders of mortgages and the shifting debtors of the banks that issue the mortgages: for in this case, no personal bonds of any sort exist."[115] One could rightly argue, of course, that even the capitalistic market economy is not an automaton and that its "rules of the game" are obvious enough to permit their subjection to moral scrutiny. Yet there is no denying that Weber's remarks point up a genuine difficulty which the Church and Catholicism faced when confronted with the "mechanics" of competitive capitalism and the prevailing "marginal morality."[116] What is more easily understood is the bitter fact that the Church for all practical purposes had by the beginning of the stage of full capitalism, disappeared from the life of most of the industrial and industrializing countries of Europe and America, that she was no longer consulted, much less listened to, by the peoples and the rulers of those countries. This is not to say that she had lost influence everywhere or that Catholic minorities in countries like England, the United States, and Germany had come to accept the notion that religion was a private affair with no bearing on public life. Actually the Catholic Church working through her members in any age and nation can be expected to make some positive contribution for the simple reason that "the charity of the Mystical Body of Christ is in itself a universal social force . . ."[117] Of course, charity while perfecting the will so as to enable man to make "social contributions," does not constrain him to do so. Social action itself is a matter of understanding and cooperation on the part of the Christians involved and also one of opportunities and circumstances.[118] It goes without saying that the degree of understanding, the circumstances and the occasions for social action differ from country to country and from period to period.

FRANZ H. MUELLER

The Social Thought of Early-American Catholics

In the United States, in postrevolutionary times, the Catholic minority—then numbering less than 25,000 in the whole land—was not confronted with serious social problems, much less with "the social question." Except for the merchants and mechanics who lived in cities like Philadelphia, these Catholics were farmers. If there was among them a consciousness of a mission of the Church in this country, it was, as Celestine J. Nuesse has shown, that of a spiritual rather than a social mission.[119] This was a consequence of the fact that the Catholics of that era were for the most part of English origin. Their spiritual leaders were still preoccupied with the doctrinal differences between Catholics and Protestants and with the evident need of their flocks for a firm mooring of their faith in dogma and personal sanctification. With their Protestant fellow countrymen, the Catholics shared the belief that religion was essential for social order.[120] But this belief was often vitiated, it seems, by undertones of bourgeois utilitarianism.[121] The emphasis was on the moral aspects of Christianity and what it allegedly does for success in life and for the preservation of the established order.[122] This in no way interfered with the practice of charity. On the contrary, personal sacrifices for the welfare of others seem at times to have enabled Catholics to ignore the broader social evils and to do so with a perfectly good conscience.[123] This is not to minimize the great amount of what Nuesse calls "personalist social action" and of organized beneficence.[124] It is simply to point out that as long as Catholics had to concentrate practically all their efforts on making a living and on surviving in an anti-Catholic atmosphere, "they were not inclined to examine critically the social and economic systems of their time." In this setting, there was indeed "no stimulus to social invention peculiar to Catholics."[125] In order not to lose out on their chances to be just as successful economically as their Protestant fellow countrymen and eventually to obtain equality of civil rights, American Catholics tended to maintain "a social outlook best described as conformist." They supported the revolution and the conservative Federalist political philosophy, and gained consequent prestige.[126] But the bourgeois ambitions and the "acquisitive appetite" especially of the more alert and leading members of their flocks caused the concern of the spiritual lead-

60

ers of early American Catholics. Father Charles Nerinckx lamented and remonstrated against the "money fever" of his prospering parishioners. Bishops Benedict J. Flaget of Bardstown, Ky., and John England of Charleston, S. C., warned against the rapidly spreading mammonism and avarice. Archbishop Ambrose Maréchal of Baltimore felt it necessary even to inform Rome that one of the special vices in which Americans indulge was "a desire for unlimited wealth which affects the mind of all . . ." There were others who condemned the growing spirit of materialism such as Fathers Anthony Kohlmann, John Hughes, Jeremiah O'Callaghan, John B. David, and laymen like Judge William Gaston, or Matthew Carey and Thomas FitzSimons who fought the idea of laissez faire.[127]

American Catholicism and Slavery

Catholic laymen were also active in the American Colonization Society which aimed to resettle freed slaves in Africa, if only for the reason that free Negroes were socially ostracized both south and north of the Mason–Dixon Line.[128] Bishop England seems to have hoped that the Church in America would provide missionaries for Liberia, then a small colony of freed United States slaves. In 1833 he wrote Rome that in the South he had to work "under a system which perhaps is the greatest moral evil that can desolate any part of the civilized world."[129] Nevertheless, while he was opposed to the continuation of slavery, he had no hope that it would be abolished. He argued that Pope Gregory XVI had not absolutely condemned slavery, that as such it was not opposed to the natural law, and that an immediate emancipation would merely create a new Negro problem. And he told Daniel O'Connell, the Irish leader, who was urging the mostly anti-Negro Irish to support abolition, to stay out of the question, as it was a matter for Americans and their legislature to decide.[130] Irishmen in this country regarded Negro labor as unfair competition and they seemed to be afraid that abolition of slavery would choke the labor market with colored would-be competitors. Bishop England declared that in his diocese Negroes were treated better than the Irish. It seems that many priests in the South kept slaves. They treated them well and were shocked by the bad treatment that Negro slaves received elsewhere. But they seem not to

61

have had any qualms of conscience about keeping and using them.[131] As a matter of fact, even the Ninth Provincial Council under the presidency of Archbishop Francis Kenrick of Baltimore in a Pastoral Letter of May, 1858, dealing with the problem, did not take any stand pro or con. It declared that the faithful in matters of policy and social order were free to follow their own informed conscience and that the clergy, in keeping with the peaceful and conservative character of the principles of the Church, have wisely refrained from getting involved in the heated agitation about domestic slavery.[132]

The Irish Laboring Poor and Catholic Colonization

Theodore Maynard has drawn attention to the fact that the Irish, who originally showed so little sympathy with the Negro, were not unaware of their own lack of freedom. Only after Southern politicians had expressed scorn for all who earned their livelihood by manual labor, did they begin to realize that their own misery was not the fault of the Negro but a consequence of a negative attitude toward labor which expressed itself both in the institution of slavery and in the depressed situation of wage labor.[133] They could see also that they themselves were regarded by native laborers as immigrant competitors, ready to work for low wages. This had applied already to the earlier groups of Irish immigrants, but became yet more apparent when, after the potato famine of 1845, the Irish arrived in great waves. "Generally poor, professing a penalized religion in the old country and finding themselves a minority in the new, it was only natural that they should ally themselves with the aspirations of common people everywhere.[134] Then as now, most of them took sides with the democratic forces in politics.[135]

It is important to keep in mind that the Irish flocked to the cities, partly because industrialization provided jobs, partly because they wished to be near to one another. Many had never been farmers in their homeland, others had had discouraging experiences with farming in Ireland, and almost all of them were too poor to migrate further inland. Bishops Loras and Crétin, and later Bishops John L. Spalding, James O'Connor, Stephan Ryan, and John Ireland made great efforts to relocate as many Irish on farms and homesteads as possible—with little success, relatively speaking.[136] Bishop Ireland's settlements did develop into prosperous farming communities, but few of the early settlers were laborers from the industrial centers of the East or from the large cities. It was not a place for poor people to start. Farmers and small businessmen from other states flocked in large numbers to the area, even farmers from within Minnesota sold their land and headed for the extraordinarily fertile land that the bishop had secured in five counties of western Minnesota from various railroad companies. Besides, the settlers were not all Irish. As James P. Shannon relates, ". . . the Irish settlers who were brought to Minnesota by various forms of 'assisted emigration' were almost universally unsuccessful," while Irish-American farmers who had gathered experience elsewhere, especially on small farms in the East, did well.[137] All in all, the Minnesota colony plan did not succeed in bringing enough Catholic people "out of the tenements of the East to relieve noticeably the social tensions in that area."[138]

The Church and American Labor

Among leading Catholics there were in the nineteenth century not a few who would solve the social question not so much by insisting on social justice as by removing the urban poor from their perilous environment, promoting temperance, and warning the laborers of the dangers of supposedly radical movements. Archbishop James R. Bayley, for instance, seriously hoped that the Irish Catholic Benevolent Union would steer the workers away from "the miserable associations called labor organizations" whose "idea is communistic."[139] The fears of bishops and priests regarding the labor movement were certainly not unfounded. During the 1870s, for instance, exploited and abused Irish immigrant laborers had gained control of some lodges of the Ancient Order of Hibernians in the anthracite region of Pennsylvania and had attempted to get justice by using violence. As "Molly Maguires" this secret organization for years terrorized the coal fields, murdering company officials, destroying property, intimidating foremen. Finally a Pinkerton detective, James McPharlan, who had posed as a desperate fugitive and worked his way up in the organization, had gathered enough evidence to enable the public

authorities to indict and convict twenty-four members—all Irish—
ten of whom were hanged for murder.[140] The public unjustly
blamed the Noble Order of the Knights of Labor, the first major
American labor organization, for the spreading industrial unrest.
The Knights originally were a secret union, whose members were
supposedly for the most part Catholics of Irish extraction. In
Canada, where the Church was under French influence, this organization was condemned and, at the urging of Cardinal Tas-
chereau of Quebec, the condemnation was sustained by the Holy
Office of the Vatican. Even the great John Lancaster Spalding,
in 1880, deplored the fact that it was almost impossible to keep the
Irish poor of the manufacturing cities out of the labor unions,
"the tendency of which in the United States will be more and
more in the direction of Communism." He considered it "folly
to imagine that trade-unions can permanently control the price
of labor."[141] He felt that unions "tend to create hatred and envy"
and little by little supplant[s] the Church."[142] Nevertheless, the
American hierarchy, though divided in their opinion about the
Knights, at the Third Plenary Council of Baltimore, meeting in
1884, decided "that priests should not, unless with the 'previous explicit authorization' of a special committee, condemn labor unions
on the ground that they were using the device of secrecy in their societies or attempting to inflict injustices upon employers."[143] The
leading American churchmen realized that if there ever was danger
of socialism and revolution in this country, it would be a result of
the suppression of the labor movement rather than of its support.
It became obvious that charitable organizations, temperance societies, or benevolent associations could not possibly solve the
problems caused by social injustice. Archbishop Gibbons of Baltimore in particular felt that any continued attempt on the part of
the ecclesiastical authorities to ignore these problems would lead
to a mass defection of workers from the Church. At his request,
Terence V. Powderly, the Irish "Grand Master Workman" of the
Knights, in 1886, explained to a committee of archbishops the
exact requirement of the pledge to be made by those who wished
to join the Knights. Their rituals and other elements of secrecy
had been abandoned some five years before. However, since two of
the archbishops remained unconvinced, the issue had to be referred to Rome for a decision.

The Church and Georgism

The whole affair coincided, more or less, with the famous McGlynn case. Father Edward McGlynn, pastor of a large New York parish, who espoused the single-tax philosophy of Henry George, had also supported the latter's candidacy for mayor of New York City. After visiting Ireland, in 1882, Henry George had published a book on the Irish Land Question in which he took the side of the Irish Land Leaguers, a fact which seems to have endeared him to a large part of the Irish population of New York. Henry George's popularity and Father McGlynn's magnetic personality worried the Democratic Party, which heretofore was assured of the unquestioned support of most of the Catholics of the area. Upon an inquiry by the chairman of Tammany Hall's Committee on Resolutions whether it was true that the Catholic clergy favored the candidacy of Henry George, the vicar general of the Archdiocese of New York assured the inquirer that the opposite was true and that George's teachings were considered contrary to the teachings of the Church. Henry George lost, but the heavy vote he had piled up won him "something of a moral victory."[144] After the election, the newly elevated Archbishop of New York, Michael A. Corrigan, supposedly at the urging of Bishop Bernard McQuaid of Rochester, N.Y., formally denounced Georgism with the result that Father McGlynn publicly and scornfully contradicted him. While McGlynn was, no doubt, truculent and recalcitrant, the archbishop's pastoral did contain passages which seemed to confirm the time-worn Marxian accusation that the Church, instead of demanding social justice of the "capitalists," counseled the employers to treat their workers charitably, and urged workers to await patiently "the rewards of eternal happiness."[145] There are indications that Cardinal Gibbons, Archbishop Ireland, Bishop John J. Keane and others, though they could hardly defend McGlynn's belligerence, much less the socialist implications of his teachings, were nevertheless unhappy about the manner in which the matter was handled in New York. There was no doubt that George had a large following among the working people and Archbishop Gibbons feared that Father McGlynn's suspension and excommunication would be looked upon by the masses as an ecclesiastical repudiation of the laboring class. The archbishop of Baltimore, as quasi-primate of the

Church of the United States, thus resolved to take the opportunity of his forthcoming visit to Rome to receive the red hat to try to convince the Holy Office that it would be unwise publicly to condemn Henry George's *Progress and Poverty*, just as it would be unjust and dangerous to denounce the Knights.

Through an indiscretion, Gibbons' memorial in behalf of the Knights, which had been drafted with the assistance of Archbishop Ireland, was published soon after it had been presented to the Prefect of the Sacred Congregation of the Propaganda, Cardinal Simeoni.[146] The intended secrecy had allowed Cardinal Gibbons to express himself most clearly and candidly, the unintended disclosure proved the Catholic Church of America to be genuinely concerned about the welfare of the proletariat. Gibbons' mission was a full success not only because the Holy See lifted the penalties that had been imposed upon the Canadian Knights and later ruled that the order could be tolerated, but also and particularly because his memorial had obviously been effective in its attempt to demonstrate that the Church's place must be on the side of labor or she would lose all influence with the masses of the workers. Both Cardinal Gibbons and Cardinal Manning of Westminster, who wholeheartedly supported Gibbons, made it plain, of course, that the need for the Church to interest herself resolutely in the grievances of the working classes, was not merely dictated by fear of their defection, but was primarily a matter of upholding social justice and of defending the dignity and rights of labor.[147]

Leo XIII and the Social Question

There can be no doubt that in defending the rights of Catholic workers to join labor unions and in averting the public condemnation of Georgism, Gibbons had done a tremendous service to the Catholic social movement in general and American Catholicism in particular. Some writers on this subject make it appear, however, that without the impetus of progressive American bishops, the Church would have remained unaware of the social question or would have answered that question in a manner that would have lost her the masses of the faithful.[148] Anyone with even a slight knowledge of social Catholicism in Austria, England, France, Germany, Italy, and even in some smaller countries of Europe is aware of the fact that in the 1880s the Catholics of these countries could already look back on a long and rich history of Catholic social movements. What is particularly important, however, is that the then reigning pope, Leo XIII, had long before the publication, in 1891, of the encyclical *Rerum novarum* (On the Conditions of Labor) concerned himself with various aspects of the social question. Even his very first encyclical, *Inscrutabili Dei* of April 21, 1878, dealt with "the present ills of society." In that document he pointed out that it was basically the contempt of a materialistic world for the authority of the Church which had undermined the very foundations of human society. Respect for the dignity and the rights of the Holy See he considered a prerequisite for the welfare of human society as a whole. Another condition indispensable for the achieving of the common good, he stated, was the restoration of the family, the germ cell of civil society. In the same year, on December 28, 1878, there appeared Leo's encyclical on socialism (*Quod apostolici muneris*) in which he demonstrated the institutions of marriage and private property to be the pillars of human society. Yet ownership, he declared, obliges: those who are prosperous are bound under pain of mortal sin to share their surplus with those in need. There are no alternatives to sharing but the relapse of society into slavery or a condition of permanent social unrest and rebellion. It is time, the pontiff added, to develop a genuine and intense interest in the organizations which indigent craftsmen and laborers have of late been forming in defense of their rights and their dignity. Even in the encyclical, *Aeterni Patris*, of August 4, 1879, which concerns itself with questions of philosophy and Catholic education, the Holy Father took the opportunity to point out how much civil society would profit from a return to those teachings of St. Thomas Aquinas that bear upon social and civic life. In *Arcanum divinae sapientiae* of February 10, 1880, he returned once more to the idea that the current desecration of matrimony will be the ruin of humanity. Where marriage is no longer regarded as a sacred bond, the family can no longer function as the nursery of obedience, the virtue to which Leo turned in his encyclical *Diuturnum illud* of June 29, 1881, treating the authority of the state. Where the divine origin of civil authority is questioned or even denied, the pope stated, there the door is opened to "those dreadful monsters of human society," the destructive philosophies of communism, socialism, and nihilism. He took it for granted and said so in the encyclical, *Humanum genus* (April 20, 1884) that, because of the similarity of their basic views, socialists and free masons will cooperate in an attempt to pervert the minds of the working people. He feared that the oppressed and discouraged members of the laboring classes would follow the alluring calls of the secret societies and masonic lodges. He called for counteraction, particularly for a Catholic effort to organize guildlike associations and fraternities where those workmen would find protection and support. Protection is needed, the pope said, particularly against the ideologies of modern liberalism. That liberalism was the topic of his encyclical, *Libertas*, of June 20, 1888. The liberals, he pointed out, were anything but liberal. There was hardly ever a school of thought more illiberal and intolerant than that of philosophical liberalism. Paradoxically, as Leo showed in *Sapientiae christianae* (January 10, 1890), it was liberalism which had brought forth one of the most coercive social agencies in human history, the modern state. In that encyclical, which spelled out the duties of Christian citizens, he demonstrated how the Leviathan-state usurped the rights of the Church, and even attempted to supplant and supersede her. Long before the totalitarian state became a reality, Leo XIII exposed the intrinsic tendency of the secularized and secularizing body politic to suppress freedom, disparage the dignity of the human person, and eventually to absorb society.

The Antecedents of Rerum Novarum

The crowning of the social encyclicals of Leo XIII (the word "social" here taken in its widest sense) was the memorable encyclical *Rerum novarum*. The antecedents of this encyclical are extremely interesting and enlightening if only for the reason that they prove the perfect timing and timeliness of this great document.

Paul Jostock, a learned historian of Catholic social thought, in his commentary on *Rerum novarum* and *Quadragesimo anno* calls to mind that these papal pronouncements were made at a time when the controversial atmosphere regarding the prevailing social and economic order began to clear up.[149] There had been heated discussions, even among Catholics, as to the role of the state in the conflict between the classes of society; as to whether the solution of the social question was to be the work of charity or of justice; as to whether the industrial system was intrinsically evil or, if at all necessary, capable of reform, etc.[150] As long as the various issues were not clearly identified, the Church could hardly be expected to define her own position in the matters concerned. Even though there was certainly never any doubt as to the principles involved, there still remained the difficult problem as to their application *hic et nunc*. Only prolonged observation and careful investigation could show how to bring these principles to bear on a concrete situation that was entirely new.

As far as this new social and economic reality was concerned, the encyclical may, as Jostock has rightly pointed out, even be looked upon as a relatively early, rather than as a late, pronouncement. While it is true that in the last decade of the nineteenth century the economic development had reached new heights, this did not mean that from there on it took a downward turn. The very opposite was true. Yet it is understandable that in view of the great technological advances made and the unheard-of expansion of manufacture and commerce, men received the notion that behind them there lay a long period of total and radical change and before them an age based on, and making the most of, past achievements. They did not and probably could not foresee that the rapid growth and improvements in industry, trade, and transportation characteristic of the nineteenth century, the "age of steam," were but a prelude to the second industrial revolution commencing at the turn of the century. It was exactly on the eve of that new machine age, founded on electricity and the internal combustion engine, and marked by a gigantic acceleration of physical production, that *Rerum novarum* appeared. Any student of social and economic history, therefore, cannot but admit that instead of belated, the encyclical was in reality unusually timely. One need only recall that it was just then that the concentration of industrial power, though still largely personal rather than corporate, began; that the process of proletarianization was gaining momentum; that the labor unions appeared in increasing numbers on the social scene; that the governments began to adopt measures designed to meet the "labor problems" emerging everywhere. In taking up such problems as the alleged increasing misery among the proletarian masses, the right of labor to organize, the Marxian program, the socialist movement, the state's duties toward labor

69

in general and protective labor legislation in particular, etc., *Rerum novarum* was anticipating the very issues that were soon to be uppermost in the minds of men.

European Pioneers of Rerum Novarum

Yet, long before those issues gave rise to concerted and continued action or agitation, designed to change the social institutions and practices in question, they had been the subject and theme of discussion among scholars, social reformers, and future leaders of the social movement. It has often been overlooked, even by Catholics, that it was by no means only and in the first place the socialists, the associationists, the cooperativists, the traditionalists, and so on, who dissented from classical economics and attacked the capitalistic system. In the second half of the nineteenth century, Catholics in almost all industrial countries gave expression to their distrust of the new economic philosophy and severely criticized the prevailing economic system for the evils it seemed to create wherever it spread. Soon small groups sprung up, particularly in France and Central Europe, which had become aware of the dangers to humanity and Christianity coming from capitalist industrialism. They gathered to inquire into the nature and causes of the modern social question and to find an answer to it.

These various study circles and round-table conferences had, in a way, paved the way for *Rerum novarum*. Pope Leo XIII himself mentioned those Catholics "worthy of all praise . . . who, understanding what the times require, have, by various enterprises and experiments endeavored to better the conditions of the working people without any sacrifice of principle" (41). There is every reason to believe that the pope had here in mind such eminent and pioneering men as, for example, the bishop of Mainz, W. E. von Ketteler (of whom Leo XIII is supposed to have once said to the Swiss social reformer, Caspar Decurtins: "He was my great predecessor" in the field of social reform), Baron von Vogelsang (Vienna), Cardinal G. Mermillod (Geneva), Albert Maria Weiss, O.P. (Fribourg in Switzerland), Count Georg von Hertling and Rev. Franz Hitze, members of the German Reichstag, Marquis René de la Tour du Pin and Count Albert de Mun of France, Charles Périn, economist at the University of Louvain, the Austrian Count Franz Kuefstein and many others. All of these men belonged to one or the other of the various Catholic research committees, councils, or conferences of Europe that made special studies of the social question and often submitted the fruits of their efforts to Rome. It seems rather likely that in Rome these reports were utilized in the preparation of *Rerum novarum*.[151] Leo XIII himself mentioned in his historic encyclical the "men of eminence [who were] meeting together for discussion, for the promotion of united action, and for practical work."

Panels and Study Circles

One of the first of these groups of Catholic social thinkers formed to examine the social question was the Geneva Alliance founded in 1870.[152] The occasion for the formation of this group, consisting mostly of European noblemen, was really the seizure of the Papal States. Yet from the beginning the group was intent on "fighting for the foundation of the social kingdom of Jesus Christ," as Bishop (later Cardinal) Mermillod, first chairman of the Alliance, expressed it. Another charter member, the Austrian Count Gustav Blome, drew attention to the fact that in the future the suppressed and persecuted papacy would have to rely more than before on the broad Catholic masses. In words similar to those used by Cardinal Manning and quoted by Cardinal Gibbons in his memorial in defense of the Knights of Labor (1887), it was pointed out that to support labor was to support the Church, which after all, was not a Church of the nobles but a Church of the people, i.e., of all classes of society. Awareness of this fact led to the formation within the Geneva Alliance of a special committee on social problems. It seems that this committee, due to the fact that a number of non-Swiss Catholics belonged to it, became the mother of numerous other European round-table conferences of Catholic students of the social question.

Bishop Mermillod, for instance, became, with Archbishop Domenico Jacobini, the cofounder of the Circolo dei studi sociali ed economiche in Rome (1881) and in 1884 cofounder of the Union catholique des études sociales et économiques at Fribourg. Counts Blome and Kuefstein of the Geneva Alliance became members of the Freie Vereinigung (Free Association) of German and Austrian Catholic social reformers, formed in 1883. The Circolo of the Italians, the Geneva Alliance of the Swiss, and

71

the Freie Vereinigung of the Germans and Austrians had their counterpart in France in the Conseil des études de l'œuvre des cercles catholique d'ouvriers founded, in 1882, by Brother Maurice Maignen of the Congregation of St. Vincent de Paul, but influenced largely by the Marquis René de la Tour du Pin and Count Albert de Mun. La Tour du Pin had been France's military attaché in Vienna, and there had become an ardent disciple of Carl von Vogelsang. The Fribourg Union was something like an international counterpart of the various national organizations.

It would take too much space to give a detailed description of each and all of these conferences. As regards their pioneer work for *Rerum novarum*, the most important of these groups were probably the Freie Vereinigung and the Union de Fribourg. The groundwork for the Freie Vereinigung was laid by the famous Bavarian Dominican A. M. Weiss, while it was organized and presided over by Prince Karl von Löwenstein (who later also joined the Order of Preachers as Father Raimund). Of its members we shall mention only some of the better-known names: Bishop Paul L. Haffner of Mainz, Father Franz Hitze, August Lehmkuhl, S.J., Dr. Georg Ratzinger, Count Georg von Hertling, Count E. Silva-Tarouca, and, of course, Carl von Vogelsang.

Factions and Schools of Social Thought

During the last half of the nineteenth century, social thinkers and reformers, Catholic as well as non-Catholic, were divided into numerous camps and groups. Some condemned the new economic system altogether, while others advocated wholehearted approval of it. Some of those who rejected capitalism suggested that it be replaced by a modern guild order, while others put their hope in some form of socialism. Among those who approved of capitalism there were many who acknowledged the need for reforms, some relying entirely on a change of mind, others expecting everything from a change of institutions. The ideological lines of demarcation often intersected in a strange manner: there were proponents of vocational representation who, like von Vogelsang, favored a more or less extensive participation of the state in the establishment of a sound social order, and there were advocates of economic liberalism who, like Charles Périn, stressed charity as the means of keeping competition within moral bounds. There was the great scholar and statesman von Hertling, who, although steeped in scholastic philosophy, was very much opposed to the alleged "medievalism" and paternalism of some Catholic social reformers, and there was Father Franz Hitze, who, although friend and assistant to the philanthropic manufacturer Brandts, hoped that the state and legislation would solve the social question.[153]

Leo XIII was by no means unacquainted with these problems and the various lines of thought regarding their resolution.[154] As papal nuncio in Brussels and on tours through England, France, and western Germany, he had acquainted himself with the social dangers of industrialism. His pastoral letters as bishop of Perugia, especially the letter on Church and Civilization (1877), show that he was well aware of the economic background of the modern social question. Yet, while he rejected the materialism which characterized the new economic order, he stressed the fact that the Church is not at all averse to scientific and technological progress. For a long time he felt that the Church alone had the mission of subduing the materialistic tendencies of the time and of mitigating the hardships that go with the birth of a new economic system. But he continued to study the views of the various schools of thought and the different ideological trends among the social thinkers of the century. According to Count Edoardo Soderini, his biographer, Leo, as Archbishop Pecci of Perugia, included in his studies the writings of Bishop E. von Ketteler and of the German (non-Catholic) economist Lujo Brentano. Ketteler, toward the end of his life, had become more and more convinced of the need of government intervention in social and economic matters, and particularly for protective labor legislation.[155] Brentano, as a firm believer in economic liberalism, had insisted that only through unionization could the labor market become truly competitive.

Divergent Views on the Role of Government

Even though there were probably noninterventionists among the Catholics of all industrial countries, they were particularly strong in France and in Belgium. Needless to say that as Catholics they could not possibly deny the competence of the state in social matters. Yet Charles Périn, whom we have previously mentioned, accorded to the public authorities and to social legislation merely the function of preventing obvious abuses and rejected any form of systematic government control. Frédéric Le Play, too, condemned governmental regulation of industry to solve labor problems. To Le Play and to Périn, the social problem was "rather a problem of morals than of institutions."[156] Disagreeing with Pére Alphonse Gratry, Abbé T. Corbière, and A. de Metz-Noblat, Catholic "liberals" of that time, Périn was unequivocally opposed to the *laissez-faire* doctrines of the classical economists. He believed that the solution of the social question lay in the universal application of Christian charity. His teachings, so George Goyau tells us,[157] provided a stimulus to the group of social Catholics known as the School of Angers. This school received its name from a congress held in October, 1890, at Angers by disciples of Périn and Le Play under the leadership of Bishop C. E. Freppel. It was a separatist congress set up with the express aim of opposing the interventionist tendencies which had been victorious at the so-called Social Work Congresses of Liège, in 1886, 1887, and September, 1890. The mouthpiece of the conservative "liberals" was *La réforme sociale* founded by Le Play in 1881 and serving as the organ of the noninterventionist Unions of Social Peace and the learned Society of Social Economy. The interventionists of the so-called Social Catholic School of Liège had been growing up around the *Association catholique,* the magazine founded as the organ of Count de Mun's Workingmen's Clubs.

The first congress of Liège was held under the presidency of the local bishop, Msgr. Doutreloux, who, in his address to it, said that he subscribed to the declaration of Bishop Bagshawe of Nottingham, that the state should intervene whenever without such intervention injustice could not be redressed or the necessary relief obtained. Périn and his followers became increasingly alarmed at what they regarded as the state socialism of the Social Catholics. At the third Congress in Liège, attended by the foremost leaders of the Catholic social movement of Europe, the pro- and the anti-interventionists clashed violently. Yet the general sentiments were obviously in favor of social legislation and insurance. A letter from Cardinal Manning to Bishop Doutreloux, in which he expressed the view that social peace was impossible without the establishment of just standards of industrial relations by legislation, roused the majority to enthusiasm. At the same time it

74

angered Bishop Freppel and the Périnites who, as previously stated, then went into secession.[158]

Other Issues

It goes without saying that these disagreements regarding the functions of government, even among high dignitaries of the Church, were rather confusing to the rank and file of Catholics. Yet there were still other issues which were in dispute. Even those who favored intervention were by no means agreed on the purpose of social legislation. Some felt that first the wage and credit system would have to be abolished before positive legislative measures of social reconstruction could be taken. Others were of the opinion that, since the wage contract is not intrinsically wrong and the taking of interest under prevailing conditions morally licit, legislation should restrict itself to protecting the rights of the workers and ameliorating their lot. The Freie Vereinigung, for instance, at its meeting in 1883 at the castle of Haid (Bohemia), adopted a resolution suggesting, indirectly, that the wage contract eventually be transformed into a contract of partnership, and recommending that industry be organized along corporate lines. In 1888, the Fribourg Union under Bishop Mermillod drew up a memorandum outlining what it regarded as the essential criteria of the prevailing economic order and presented it to Pope Leo XIII.[159] Following, to some extent, in the footsteps of the "Haider Theses," the Union catholique tried to show that the social evils of the time were rooted in the fundamental fallacies of capitalism, particularly its individualism. As a consequence of the prevailing egoism, labor had been reduced to a mere commodity and was regarded as merely an item in the accounting of the cost of production; property had emancipated itself from the moral law and had become an end in itself; trade and commerce, instead of regarding it as their main objective to link producer and consumer, had made profit their ultimate end. The profit economy, it was said, is based on the credit system which admits of fixed interest that can be obtained only by a corresponding reduction of wages. An economic system, however, whose cornerstone is exploitation and usury cannot but destroy the social equilibrium and pave the way for the downfall of civilization. Because it is fundamentally wrong, this system cannot be improved, it can only be replaced by a new, a corporative system.

This memorandum in practically all of its statements and formulations bespeaks the spirit of Carl von Vogelsang. This is not surprising if one keeps in mind that the three founders of the Fribourg Union, Counts Blome and Kuefstein, and the Marquis René de la Tour du Pin were all pupils and enthusiastic disciples of von Vogelsang.[160] It is only fair, though, to state that the Fribourg Union, as far as the ethics of the wage contract was concerned, accepted the advice of Augustine Lehmkuhl, S.J. This German moral philosopher had severely criticized the views of von Vogelsang, A. M. Weiss, O.P., and other representatives of the Freie Vereinigung regarding wage justice and interest. He granted that a "society contract" (partnership) would conform best with Christian charity, but he denied emphatically that it is demanded by justice.[161]

The "Roman Theses"

Emil Ritter, a historian of German political Catholicism, has drawn attention[162] to the fact that Lehmkuhl's attitude in the matter resembled in many respects that of the Circolo dei studi sociali ed economiche in Rome which had been convoked at the request of the Vatican by the secretary of the Propaganda Fide, Archbishop (later Cardinal) Jacobini. To this circolo there belonged such men as Archbishop (later Cardinal) G. Mermillod[163], Prof. S. Talamo, an eminent Thomist, who was largely responsible for the formulation of the "theses" of this commission, H. Denifle, O.P., Matteo Liberatore, S.J., Count Kuefstein, and a number of other distinguished priests and laymen. Two of them, Dr. K. Lugmayer and Abbé A. Villeneuve, of Canada, must be credited with having petitioned the Holy See to appoint just such a committee. The theses of the circolo are of special importance since there are strong indications that one of its authors, the Jesuit Liberatore (in addition to Cardinal Zigliara, O.P.) was confidential adviser to Leo XIII and assisted him in the drafting of the labor encyclical.

If one compares the statements and memoranda of the Fribourg Union and of the Freie Vereinigung with the propositions advanced by the circolo, the difference between the reformatory zeal of the former and the sober and more positive attitude of the latter becomes at once obvious. The "Roman Theses" state, *inter alia*:

> Because the exchange value of the product of labor can be expressed in terms of money, it is also possible to set a price on labor itself . . .
>
> The earnings of any economic enterprise consist of three parts: the first belongs to the worker, the second to the enterpriser or manager, the third to the capitalist. The entrepreneur divides the shares according to agreement (contract) and acquired (vested) rights. If a business undertaking is unable to satisfy the minimum needs of the three "partners" in the enterprise (just named), it does not accomplish its economic purpose and, thus, forfeits its right to exist. Since the worker ordinarily depends for his living on the returns from his labor, he has a prior claim upon the earnings of the employer for whom he works . . . The owner(s) of the working assets or of the capital of the enterprise in question should obtain what suffices to secure his (their) continued cooperation . . . This is in the interest of society. For in this manner, the value of property is preserved, people stimulated to save, and an incentive provided for people to stay in business and to add new enterprises to the old . . .
>
> Money serves two purposes: It is a standard of value facilitating exchange of commodities or of their equivalents, and it is a store of value facilitating the accumulation and disbursement of purchasing power. It is permissible to derive pecuniary advantages from the following uses of money: Exchanging it for things the use of which can be evaluated apart from the thing itself [rent?]; buying government bonds; transacting business with it; investing it by way of partnership in other people's enterprises; lending it at interest at the legal or prevailing rate.[164]

These samples may suffice to demonstrate that the *circolo* was more intent on clarifying the facts of the situation and its socio-ethical possibilities than on a radical reorganization of the social economy. This does not mean, however, that the Roman Study Circle was definitely opposed to reform. But in recognizing certain historical developments as not intrinsically vicious but rather capable of serving the common good, it gave encouragement to immediate legislative action particularly for the purpose of protecting the rights and improving the living and working conditions of laboring men. It is probably true that the more decidedly anti-capitalistic attitude of the Fribourg Union with its all-inclusive distant goals did not provide sufficient motivation for social legislation serving proximate ends.

Rerum Novarum and the Schools of Social Thought

Did *Rerum novarum* follow the line of so-called social romanticism as exemplified by von Vogelsang and A. M. Weiss, or the line of "realism" as exemplified by A. Lehmkuhl and M. Liberatore? Did it endorse the views of the School of Liège or those of the School of Angers? Did it merely tolerate the institution of interest and of wage labor or did it approve of them? Did it favor vocational corporations, representing both employers and employees, or did it approve wholeheartedly of outright labor unions?

No attempt will be made to answer all these questions. Actually, the encyclical did not expressly endorse or condemn any of the various Catholic schools of social thought nor any of the factions of the Catholic social movement. Instead, it reaffirmed the traditional social doctrines of the Church, applying them, in a general way, to the new social problems of the time.

It is true, however, that when the encyclical appeared, not a few spokesmen of the disputing groups were quick in pointing out certain of its phrases and passages as supposedly vindicating their own points of view. Pope Leo XIII, however, never identified himself with any of those particular lines of thought, not even when they were identical with the teachings of his labor encyclical. This must, of course, not be interpreted to mean that Leo took no interest in the controversy or that he ignored the divergent views. On the contrary, the encyclical makes it a point to define the position of the Church relative to the "doctrinal" issues concerned. Yet there can be no doubt that the primary concern of the author of the encyclical was to answer the practical questions arising from the then prevailing "conditions of the working classes." Leo XIII, obviously, did not intend to propose, much less to outline, a reorganization of the social economy. The conditions of the working classes were such as to necessitate an immediate rescue operation. There is no sense in presenting flood victims in immediate danger of losing life and possessions with a blueprint of postdiluvial reconstruction plans. Similarly, in 1891, workers would have received little encouragement from a plan for national economic councils and functional representation or some similar program of social reform. Besides, there was no hope whatsoever that the statesmen and businessmen of the time, captivated as they were by the seeming successes of the policy of *laissez faire*, would have as much as taken notice of such reform proposals. "The 'idols of Liberalism,' " as George G. Higgins has rightly pointed out, "had to be overturned before the more fully developed program of 'reconstructing social order' . . . could be successfully launched."[165] Unbelievable as it may seem to the present generation, there was even need to prove to some, if not the very existence, then at least the seriousness, of the social question. *Rerum novarum*, thus, undertook to determine the nature of the ills of modern society, to trace their causes, to point out the necessity and urgency of a solution, to identify the problems which called for immediate action, and to indicate the proper remedies for the social ills in question.

No, Leo did not follow the line of social romanticism but neither did he "realistically" accept the prevailing socioeconomic order as a basically unalterable fact. Nobody needed to convince him of the need for and the possibility of a change. He did share with the Réforme sociale school of Angers a firm belief in the right of association, in the need for self-restraint, and in the social efficacy of charity. Whether he gradually "veered" in the direction of the Liège school of the Association catholique, as has been said, is open to question.[166] Both schools accepted the principle of government intervention, but the school of Angers (Périn, Freppel, Le Play) wanted it limited to legal protection and the repression of abuses while the school of Liège (de Mun, de la Tour du Pin, Doutreloux) favored a more active role of the state—but largely of the counterrevolutionary corporative state, not the centralist and individualist state created by the French Revolution.[167]

Leo XIII and the Social Function of Government

Leo definitely acknowledged it to be a function of government to protect the workers against the abuses of a ruthlessly individualistic capitalism. But the encyclical contains no recommendation of social legislation going beyond protective labor legislation. In connection with a discussion of the association of workingmen as well as Catholic benefit and insurance societies, the pope says: "Among the purposes of a society should be to try to arrange for a continuous supply of work at all times and seasons; and to create a fund from which the members may be helped in their necessities, not only in case of accident but also in sickness, old age, and misfortune" (3). Actually, the pope never tires of emphasizing that "man is older than the state" and that the domestic society, the family, is anterior both in idea and in fact to civil society "with rights and duties of its own, totally independent of the commonwealth" (9). Thus the state may neither abolish nor absorb paternal authority. However, the pope acknowledges, strictly in keeping with what is now called the principle of subsidiarity, that "if a family finds itself in great difficulty, utterly friendless, and without prospect of help, it is right that extreme necessity be met by public aid." The same is true, "if within the walls of the household there occur grave disturbances of mutual rights." It appears like an answer to the present-day demands for Federal aid to education, when the pope states that the socialists, "in setting aside the parent and introducing the providence of the state, act *against natural justice*, and threaten the very existence of family life" (11).

After rejecting the teachings of socialism and, implicitly, of any brand of collectivism, the pope proceeds to outline the principles of a Christian solution. To those who feel that all that is needed is "enlightened" laws to change prevailing institutions and environment, he says: "let men try as they may, no strength and no artifice will ever succeed in banishing from human life the ills and troubles which beset it" (14).

One need only recall the rapid development of totalitarianism after the First World War in order to understand why Leo XIII, whenever he emphasizes the duty of the state to assist in the solution of labor problems, adds a warning or qualification. Exactly because the state *is* the most perfect natural society and its authority so far-reaching, its political power is peculiarly subject to abuse. That is why the pope again warns that "the state must not absorb the individual citizen or the family; both should be allowed free and untrammeled action as far as is consistent with the common good and the interest of others" (28). As a matter of fact, the state should protect the freedom of the citizens. If, for example, "employers laid burdens upon workmen which were unjust, or degraded them with conditions that were repugnant to their dignity as human beings . . . it would be right to call in the help and authority of the law." Again, without naming it so, the pope refers to the principle of subsidiarity by saying that "the limits must be determined by the nature of the occasion which calls for the law's interference—the principle being this, that the law must not undertake more, nor go further, than is required for the remedy of the evil or the removal of the danger" (29). It is understandable that in an age of *laissez faire*, social reformers stressed the fact that *Rerum novarum* acknowledged the part which the state has to play in the solution of the social question. However, believing their cause to be vindicated, some interventionists overlooked or passed over the equally important fact that the same encyclical takes pains to show that the functions of the state are essentially subsidiary, that is to say, supplementary. Those of our supposedly "liberal" contemporaries, who wish to develop the state into a kind of Universal Aunt cannot possibly claim Leo XIII as their supporter. No doubt, "the Pope explicitly approves factory legislation and other provisions to secure good conditions of labor," but "he is careful to remark that the state should step in only when employers and employed fail to come to a satisfactory agreement."[168] He states in so many words that in regard to hours, working conditions, etc., "it is advisable that recourse be had to Societies or Boards" to be approved of and protected by the state, but otherwise autonomous, "in order to supersede undue interference on the part of the government"(34). It is here that the pope no longer restricts himself to defending the natural rights of workmen but urges the formation of vocational groups, labor unions and industry councils (36), even though he does not, as yet, propose total social reconstruction in terms of functional representation.

The Quintessence of Rerum Novarum

If one would have to epitomize *Rerum novarum* to the barest minimum and yet use the encyclical's own words, perhaps the following quotations would best summarize its most important concerns:

1. "Whenever the general interest or any particular class suffers, or is threatened with evils which can in no other way be met, the public authority must step in to meet them" (28).

2. "But the rulers of the state must go no further: nature bids them to stop here" (11).

3. ". . . employers and workmen may themselves effect much in the matter [viz., the solution of the social question], by means of . . . institutions and organizations . . . the most important of which are workmen's associations . . ." (36). "To enter into [a] society of this kind is a natural right of man, which the state must protect" (38).

Recognition of Labor Unions

Leo XIII, thus, recognized the existence of the social question and acknowledged the need for its speedy solution, recommending self-help through labor organizations and, where voluntary organization and measures proved insufficient, governmental, especially legal, measures. In all likelihood, credit for the Church's recognition of the labor unions should go to Cardinal Gibbons. Recent archival studies on the preparation of the text of *Rerum novarum* seem to show that Leo XIII in the last minute before publication personally made a little, yet significant, change. Originally, we are told, Section 36 of the encyclical referred only to guildlike organizations consisting of employers and employees (mixed corporations). This was changed to read "[societies] consisting either of workmen alone, or of workmen and employers together."[169] Gérard Dion, M.S.S., expressed the opinion that the original phrasing was due to the influence of those European groups which supported a return to the guild system.[170] Actually, Leo XIII already in his encyclical, *Humanum genus*, seven years earlier, expressed himself in favor of guildlike organizations. Yet neither he nor any of the study circles that did preparatory work for the encyclicals supported a return to medieval institutions. Even those groups that showed medievalistic inclinations and proposed a corporative state, were rather anxious to point out that they did not envisage any "repristination" of the vocational fraternities of the Middle Ages. Besides, the guilds did not originally comprise employers and employees. Journeymen and apprentices, who were under the protection of the guild, were not "employees" in the modern sense, but students of a craft and assistants to a guild master, rather than wage earners. Nevertheless, those nineteenth-century Catholic social thinkers who favored organizations which included both employers ("masters") and the employees may rightfully be assumed to have either been unaware of the positive significance of the unions or unable to see their historical necessity. Others probably rejected them together with capitalism, considering them part and parcel of that system. But we must not forget that even many leading American Catholics, among them liberal-minded bishops, felt uneasy about, or were afraid of, unions. Thus, if Gibbons and, as some assume, Manning, did convince Leo XIII of the importance and salutary functions of unions, they certainly deserve our gratitude. Even those who have misgivings about more recent unionism can hardly deny that absence or an abolition of unions would eventually have lead to a class war of a kind hitherto practically unknown in the United States. For men, as Cardinal Gibbons wrote years after *Rerum novarum*, "are apt to conspire in secret if not permitted to express their views openly. The public recognition among us of the right to organize implies a confidence in the intelligence and honesty of the masses; it affords them an opportunity of training themselves in the art of self-government and the art of self-discipline; it takes away from them every excuse and pretext for the formation of dangerous societies, . . ."[171]

Catholic Union Leadership in America

Socialists have claimed, rightly or wrongly, that around the turn of the century Bishop James E. Quigley of Buffalo attempted to organize Catholic unions, as Section 40 of *Rerum novarum* did seem to suggest.[172] Whether or not Quigley needed to be persuaded by Catholic labor leaders to give up his plans, if any, there is probably some truth in the statement by David J. Saposs, a socialist, that there was no need for Catholic trade unions because Catholics became ever more influential in the American labor movement.[173] It is probably an overstatement to say, as Saposs does, that the American Federation of Labor, successor to the Knights, was primarily an immigrant organization. But it is quite likely that the second generation of the Irish immigrant laborers moved up into the ranks of the skilled workers and entered the A. F. of L., consisting of craft unions, in increasing numbers. As faithful Catholics, who felt that their bishops backed them up, they battled the socialist members in the Federation, who at one time (1894/95) put John McBride of the United Mine Workers, a typical industrial union, into the presidency of the Federation. Father Peter E. Dietz, one-time editor of the German-American Catholic Central Verein's *Central-Blatt and Social Justice*, at the St. Louis convention of the A. F. of L. in 1910, gathered the Catholic trade union delegates into an organization which he called the Militia of Christ for Social Service.[174] The purpose of the Militia was to counteract the socialists' persistent endeavor to gain control of the A.F. of L., but counteracting, not so much by attacking socialism, as by engendering among American Catholics a growing sense of responsibility toward the labor movement and by urging Catholic workmen to join the unions affiliated with the A. F. of L.[175] Whether or not as a consequence of Father Dietz's persistent and spirited efforts, there can be no doubt that Catholics gradually came into the ascendancy in many unions, except, perhaps, in the Railroad brotherhoods and needle trades.[176] An amazingly high percentage of Irish Catholic unionists reached and still occupy leading positions in the American labor movement, especially in its A. F. of L. sector. There has never been since *Rerum novarum* a dearth of workmen's priests in America, from Irish-born Father Peter C. Yorke of San Francisco to Father John M. Corridan, S.J., the waterfront priest in the East, son of an Irish-born New York policeman, who was particularly active in the decade after World War II.[177] Many of the labor priests devoted, and still devote, their time and energy to educational work in labor schools, industrial relations institutes, and associations of Catholic unionists. Among the scores of priest-educators who have done and are doing a tremendous amount of demanding, yet mostly unpublicized, work in this field are such men as Msgr. Daniel M. Cantwell of Chicago, Msgr. Francis J. Gilligan of St. Paul, and Father William J. Smith, S.J., of Jersey City. A particularly gratifying aspect of this type of adult education is that it provides leadership training, badly needed in the continuous fight against labor racketeering, and it acquaints the unionists with the social teachings of the Church. At times when the unions have come under fire because of corruption and a lack of civic-mindedness in some sectors of the movement, these schools, by imbuing unionists with a sense of responsibility toward the common good, have done an inestimable service to labor.

European Allies

It is only fair in this connection to draw attention to the pioneer work done in this field by the Catholic Workers' College in Oxford, England, envisaged since 1909 by Charles Plater, S.J., and made a reality in 1921 through the initiative of the Catholic Social Guild and the generosity of the English Jesuits who released the able Leo O'Hea, S.J., to become the first principal of the College.[178] A few years later, the Belgian Jeunesse ouvrier Chrétienne (Jocists) under the zealous leadership of Canon Joseph Cardijn started experimenting with workers' education through the medium of study circles for young Catholic workers. The success of this movement is established by the fact that it is rapidly spreading all over the world.[179] In this country it is known as Y.C.W., and until recently was under the presidency of the competent and idealistic Michael J. Coleman, Jr., one-time assistant to Msgr. George G. Higgins, Director of the Social Action Department of the National Catholic Welfare Conference.

Msgr. John T. Ellis relates that, in 1925, Pope Pius XI expressed deep sorrow to Canon Cardijn about the Church's loss of the working classes in Europe in the nineteenth century. The distinguished historian feels that this calamity never befell the Church in the United States because of men like Gibbons who were able to convince workingmen of the sincere friendship of the Church.[180] If the Church in Europe was less successful in this respect, it was not, however, because of a lack of understanding of the social question on the part of Catholic leaders. In those critical years, the voice of bishops and Catholic social reformers did not reach the powers that were. But with regard to the United States, Prof. Ellis is probably right that in the latter part of the nineteenth century a bond was forged between the American hierarchy and the Catholic laboring men which has proved strong enough not only to resist repeated attacks by leftist and anti-Christian forces but also to "hold" in a time when the labor movement no longer needed the powerful and energetic support of the Church and when the Church itself was no longer considered the refuge of impoverished immigrants and the shelter for the urban proletariat.

The Issue of Labor Legislation

If *Rerum novarum* had stimulated the growth of unionism in the United States or at least encouraged the wholehearted co-operation of American Catholics in the labor movement, the same can hardly be said of legislative social policy. This is not to say that there was no awareness among Catholic leaders of the need for governmental intervention in behalf of the laboring class. Aaron I. Abell, who might well be called *the* historian of the Catholic social movement in the United States, maintains that at least in the decade after *Rerum novarum*, many if not most Catholics favored compulsory arbitration.[181] The Baltimore Catholic Congress of 1889—two years before *Rerum novarum*—declared "civil enactments" to be necessary to solve the conflict between capital and labor. William Richards, a Washington lawyer, in a paper presented at the congress, expressed the opinion that unions, while justified as defense organizations of labor, are by nature somewhat self-centered and should, therefore, be supplemented by a social insurance system of the Bismarckian type.[182] Peter L. Foy of St. Louis, one of the leaders of that lay congress, in a paper composed at the request of an advisory committee of bishops, also stressed the need for insurance and for state aid especially for the marginal laborers.[183] The Columbian Catholic Congress of 1893 held in Chicago in connection with the world's fair expressed itself in a similar vein,[184] as a matter of fact, its plea for state intervention was even stronger.[185] At its fifty-fourth convention in Indianapolis in 1906, even the somewhat more conservative German Roman Catholic Central Verein of North America went on record as favoring not only the wage earners' right to organize, but also "more progressive labor legislation."[186]

Until World War I all these endeavors remained without practical legislative effect in the United States. Some of the states of this country had, it is true, passed a few protective labor laws before continental European countries did. Otherwise, however, American labor legislation lagged far behind Europe and so did social insurance legislation. Consciousness of the fact that the prevailing competitive economic order was the prize of victory over the command economy of British mercantilism was, it seems, still strong, at least in the minds of legislators and judges. Long periods of relative prosperity, the tenacious opposition of the employers, and the critical attitude of the Supreme Court also account for the slow and piecemeal development of social legislation in the United States. Practically every law that did pass the reluctant legislative bodies was challenged in the courts, because these laws were looked upon as restricting the right of contract and seizing property without due process of law, not to speak of the possible invasion of state rights. It was not until the beginning of the Great Depression that American public opinion and the Supreme Court became more amenable to this type of legislation.[187]

The Other Side of the Coin

Even though England and most continental European countries were considerably ahead of the United States as far as protective labor laws and social insurance were concerned, it should not be taken for granted that this was all to the good of the "progressive" nations of Europe. In Germany, which, since Bismarck's reforms, had taken the lead, the comprehensive social insurance program probably delayed the democratization process. Bismarck introduced it not so much to solve the social question as to bribe the workers away from Marxian internationalism and to attach them securely to the new German Empire. The consequent governmentalization of the German mind doubtless reduced its power of resistance to the totalitarian ideology which engulfed the German nation in 1933. It is significant that German Catholic social thinkers originally shied away from comprehensive "social" security systems which they realized were actually governmental security systems, that is, tax-supported and not based on genuine insurance principles. They did so even after they had acknowledged, not without difficulty, that state and government do have important functions with regard to the social order.

Corporatism or Meliorism?

For a long time, German and Austrian Catholic social thinkers had felt that some kind of a modernized guild order was the only promising answer to the social question, that is, a socioeconomic order based on autonomous vocational corporations.[188] It is Bishop W. E. von Ketteler who must be credited with the gradual reorientation of social Catholicism of Germany toward governmental social policy. He never wavered in his belief in a corporate social order, but in his later years he began to realize that such an order can hardly be accomplished without, much less against, the state. What is more, however, is the fact that he now acknowledged, more than ever before, a Christian responsibility toward immediate social problems which, he felt, could not be solved without a strong union movement and without state intervention. As a matter of fact, even the corporate reorganization of the working classes was no longer thought of as a complete change of the prevailing socioeconomic order, but as an attempt to incorporate or integrate the workers in that order, giving them status and dignity. Since, however, it was the state, the bishop said, which had deprived the workers of their rights, "it is the duty of the state to restore the legal protection of labor."[189] In a paper presented to his brother bishops at the Fulda Conference of the German hierarchy in 1869, and again in his draft of a political program, published in 1873 as "The Catholics in the German Empire," Ketteler demanded prohibition of child labor in factories, limitation of working hours for minors, a maximum working day, Sunday rest, compensations for disabled workers, a law protecting and favoring workers' cooperatives, factory inspection, and so on.[190] For a short time member of the German Reichstag, Ketteler even drafted a bill which aimed at a further development of the then existing federal protective labor legislation. While this first draft was not submitted to the legislature, it seems likely that Ketteler's initiative provided the impetus for the famous Bill Galen (1877), the first comprehensive legislative program of the Center Party for the protection of factory workers.[191]

Protective Labor Legislation or Social Insurance?

In the very same year, Leo XIII as Archbishop Pecci of Perugia issued his pastoral letter on Church and Civilization which shows its author to be well aware of the modern social question. Since we know through Leo's biographer, Count Edoardo Soderini, that even before his election to the Chair of Peter, Leo had studied the writings of Bishop von Ketteler, it seems legitimate to assume that Leo was aware of the fact that Ketteler had come to the conclusion that cooperation in the solution of the social question was both a necessity and a duty on the part of civil government. It is worthy of notice that neither Leo in *Rerum novarum*, nor Ketteler in what he called his sociopolitical testament propose social insurance. This does not, of course, necessarily mean that they rejected on principle any governmental scheme of protection of low-income groups against such risks as occupational disease, ill health, unemployment, etc. Protective labor legislation, at any rate, restricted the freedom of enterprise in the interest of social welfare, while tax-supported social security did not seem directly to interfere with the then predominant philosophy and policy of *laissez faire*. Bismarck, though rejecting *laissez faire*, was unyieldingly opposed to all factory legislation because he felt that it would "kill the goose which lays the golden eggs," that is, interfere with the growth and competitive ability of heavy industry, the backbone of national defense.[192] The Center Party in the Reichstag, however, kept on presenting protective labor bills to the growing distress of the Iron Chancellor, who had—as was pointed out before—set his mind on governmental "insurance" of the workers against illness, industrial accidents, disablement, and old age.

Franz Hitze, the John Ryan of Germany

In those years there arrived on the historical scene in Germany a young priest, Franz Hitze, destined to become the champion of social legislation in the German parliament. The role which Father (later Monsignor, and professor at the University of Münster in Westfalen) Hitze played in the history of governmental social policy in the three decades preceding World War I is amazingly similar to the role played by Father John A. Ryan (later Monsignor and professor at the Catholic University of America) during, and in the decades following, World War I, except that Ryan was not a member of Congress. Though an academic teacher of Catholic social thought, Hitze was a politico, more interested in practical results than in academic speculations. By the time he entered the political scene, social insurance was, for all practical purposes, a historical reality which even Hitze's more conservative colleagues in the Center Party of the Reichstag could no longer undo. Under the circumstances, Hitze felt it his duty to help make the best of the situation, refining, improving, and revising legislative proposals as well as laws already in force. Count Georg von Hertling, professor of scholastic philosophy, later chancellor of the German Empire and prime minister of Prussia, was distressed about the apparent pragmatism of his clerical fellow parliamentarian, even calling him a state socialist. The difference of opinion within the party leadership, however, soon receded into the background when Bismarck resigned and the young Emperor, William II, decided to sponsor protective labor legislation. The famous imperial rescript of February, 1890, called for an international convention to effect cooperation of the industrialized countries in the field of factory legislation and directed the secretaries of commerce and transportation of the empire to improve the existing code of regulations governing industry to include provisions protecting the health and physical safety of the workers, regulating their hours of work, taking care of their economic needs, and according them legal equality. Of particular interest, however, is the fact that the emperor sent a special messenger to Father Hitze inviting him to join the council of state which was to be convened for the purpose of implementing the imperial messages. William II sent a cordial and respectful message and a copy of the program of the international convention to Leo XIII and invited the archbishop of Breslau, Cardinal Kopp, to attend the convention as an imperial delegate. The pope replied just as kindly, and in a special message to the archbishop of Cologne, Philip Krementz, called upon the clergy and laity in Germany to cooperate in the work of social reconstruction. The German bishops in a joint pastoral letter urged the faithful to comply with the express wish of the Holy Father. The International Catholic Social Work Congress at Liège in September, 1890, with the bishops attending, encouraged by a letter from Cardinal Manning, enthusiastically endorsed the idea of social legislation, especially, however, the idea of an international agreement on protection of workers from the dangers of factory labor. It was at that time that the anti-interventionists withdrew from the Liège congress to hold a rival meeting at Angers. A few months later, Leo's magna charta of the social order, Rerum novarum, appeared. It settled the issue, the Pope stating clearly that it was the duty of government to protect the rights and the dignity of labor.

Church and State in Europe

The positive turn of social Catholicism toward the state, initiated and encouraged by the encyclical, cannot be overestimated. It is important to remember that in Italy the Papal states had been seized; in France, after the abrogation of the Napoleonic concordat with Rome and the emergence of the laicistic state, the Church was being oppressed and deprived of much of her property; in England the "disabilities of Catholics" continued to exist; in Germany the Kulturkampf had for a long time paralyzed the Church and relegated Catholics to a position of second-class citizens. It testifies to the prudence, the civic spirit, and the sense of social responsibility of the European Catholics that all these bitter experiences did not prevent them from acknowledging the office and function of government in restoring and safeguarding the welfare of society. Actually, they did more than that. It is no exaggeration to say that they not only cooperated in the work of social reconstruction but also joined in the leadership of that work. It is to the credit of the Church that of all possibilities and opportunities, her members in Europe chose the job of alleviating the conditions of the working classes as a means of reconciliation with the state. In this manner, Cardinal Manning led England's Catholics "out of the catacombs," and Bishop von Ketteler, the German Catholics out of the ghetto.[193]

The Church, Labor, and Citizenship in USA

In America no serious conflict between Church and state existed. American Catholicism had indeed "upon the whole been successful in keeping the working classes in the Church,"[194] but the government was hardly aware of the fact that keeping them in the Church meant also keeping them in the nation, shielding them from Marxian internationalism, and imbuing them with a healthy love of their country. Europeans have often been puzzled by the fact that Marxism has been least successful in the country generally recognized as the most capitalistic. When Werner Sombart, one of the world's leading experts in Marxian thought and the movement as a whole, wrote his little classic *Warum gibt es in den Vereinigten Staaten keinen Sozialismus?* ("Why is there No Socialism in the United States?")[195] he mentioned among other things the standard of living, prosperity, the democratic way of life, and the labor union movement as reasons why Marxism made almost no progress in this country. He was unaware, however, of the role played by the Catholic Church in American society. He did not realize that by championing the cause of the working classes and by supplying leadership for the labor union movement she was depriving socialism of much of its persuasive power. Sombart could have hardly suspected this in a country traditionally Protestant.

Urban and Rural Catholicism in America

Sociologists and economic historians have time and again pointed out that because their immigrant ancestors had been economically more or less forced to settle in the cities and industrialized—or industrializing—regions of this country most American Catholics are to be found in the heavily urbanized parts of the United States.[196] This is particularly true of the Irish-American Catholics. Catholic immigrants from Germany, especially those who came after 1865, preferred to settle in the same farming regions in which earlier German colonists, that is, those who had arrived in the eighteenth and early nineteenth century, had taken up their abode.[197] What C. J. Nuesse says of the German Catholics who settled in Pennsylvania in the beginning of the eighteenth century, namely, that clinging to their own language and national customs they willingly left public affairs to other nationalities such as the Irish, probably applies also to later Catholic immigrants from Germany.[198] Though it is true that many Germans did remain in such metropolitan areas as St. Louis, Milwaukee, and Cincinnati, it seems that the larger percentage of those who moved into the agricultural areas of the "German belt," as opposed to those who stayed in the cities, were Catholics. Living on scattered farms was neither conducive to learning the language of the adopted country nor to a lively participation in political affairs. Both as farmers of some means and as Germans, they tended to be conservative. Naturally, they did not share the animus against England which the Irish felt.[199] Many of them had not experienced, and were not then experiencing, the economic hardships that their Irish fellow Catholics had experienced. As urban laborers the latter flocked to the Democratic Party and to the labor unions. When self-help, such as provided by the union movement, did not seem to suffice to bring about quick improvement of their socioeconomic conditions, they were ready to appeal to the government and to demand intervention and provision of security.

Rerum Novarum's Echo in America

Yet in spite of the liberal trend among urban Catholics, the echo of Rerum novarum was, it seems, not quite what one might have expected. Individual bishops, as, for instance, John J. Keane and John Lancaster Spalding, responded to the encyclical. Spalding now revised his earlier opposition to labor unions, endorsing them, though not without qualification.[200] Some bishops apparently felt that the encyclical vindicated their long-held views. But, there was, surprisingly, no joint pastoral letter of the American hierarchy.[201] Right after the appearance of the encyclical a gratifying response arose in Catholic periodicals on the part of lay leaders, but this did not initiate a Catholic social movement. As in the past and for some time to come, social Catholicism in this country remained the concern of personalities. As Father Vincent A. McQuade, O.S.A., reports, there was in the years following the publication of Rerum novarum "a marked decrease in interest in the Encyclical and little attention devoted to the program contained in its pages."[202] One magazine felt it necessary to state that there is "no excuse for the Catholic who has not read and studied the Encyclical . . ."[203] Frederick P. Kenkel, who was to become one of America's great social leaders, two years after his conversion and some months after the labor encyclical had been issued, found no Catholic groups in Chicago organizing to actualize Rerum novarum. "Not only were Catholics not organizing, but many refused to acknowledge that the social problem depicted by Leo XIII existed in the United States."[204] "The belief was current that these problems were of lesser import in America: the expansion of industry and the westward migration seem to have influenced this view."[205] In the wake, but hardly as a consequence, of Rerum novarum, there were movements for interdenominational cooperation, for the improvement of housing conditions, for the promoting of temperance. Many Catholic clubs as well as philanthropic and charitable societies were formed. But to call all this a "battle for social liberalism," as has been suggested, seems either to give it too roseate an interpretation or to use the term "liberalism" too broadly. And where was the "battle"?

John A. Ryan, Catholic Social Leader in the Making

While Kenkel, son of German immigrants, was searching for the few who appreciated the worth of Leo's program, and to whose voices he could join his own,[206] a young candidate for the priesthood, John A. Ryan, son of Irish immigrants, intensely interested in the labor question, envisaged himself as becoming one of the "actors in a great social drama," the like of which, he firmly believed, "has not been enacted in the nineteenth Century . . ." (entry in his diary for December 11, 1892).[207] John Augustine Ryan's parents had come from Tipperary county. His mother's family had been driven from their farm and so had been his paternal grandfather's family. William and Mary Luby Ryan had settled in Vermillion, some 20 miles south of St. Paul. They subscribed to the *Irish World and American Industrial Liberator*, a paper not only staunchly Irish but also zealously devoted to social justice, supporting social legislation as well as such labor movements as the Knights of Labor. It seems, however, that reading the *Irish World* and later, as a seminarian, whatever books on social problems he could get his hands on, merely confirmed his innate zeal for social justice. It is significant that even so eager a seeker after a better social and economic order as John Ryan did not come across *Rerum novarum* until 1894, when he was almost 25 years old, and the encyclical had been published for nearly three years! It is interesting to see that young Ryan, very much like young Hitze in Germany some twenty years earlier, did not find the study of philosophy as exciting and thought-provoking as that of current social problems.[208] In 1900, he broke into print with a review of a book on strikes.[209] In 1902, he published part of his licentiate dissertation (1900) on the ethical aspects of speculation in the *International Journal of Ethics*.[210] In the April, 1903, issue of the *American Catholic Quarterly Review*, we find an

94

article by Ryan on the morality of labor unions. But it was his doctoral dissertation, published as a book, A *Living Wage: Its Ethical and Economic Aspects* (New York: Macmillan, 1906), that moved Ryan into the ranks of America's leading Catholic social thinkers.

John Ryan and the Central Verein

Leaders in Catholic social thought in those days were few and far between. And there were no followers to speak of, no Catholic social movement, except, perhaps, the German Roman Catholic Central Verein of America. It was in the latter organization that John A. Ryan was to find his first real "audience."[211] In 1908 the Central Verein had formed a special Committee for Social Propaganda, and received an encouraging letter from Archbishop John Ireland of St. Paul, saying: "I approve fully of the project of the Central Verein and wish it every success. The day has come when our Catholics, priests and laymen, must busy themselves more than they have been doing with social questions."[212] It is somewhat surprising that Father Patrick W. Gearty, who wrote *the* book on Ryan—not a biography, it is true, but a rather comprehensive presentation of his teachings—makes no reference to Ryan's early close cooperation with the Central Verein, the many articles published in the Verein's magazine, Ryan's lecture series in the Verein's workshops and seminars, his keynote address at the Fordham University meeting of the Verein in 1912, and Ryan's booklet, "A Minimum Wage by Legislation," published in 1911 by the Verein's Central Bureau in St. Louis. Ryan himself in his autobiography, *Social Doctrine in Action* (1941), put the name of Frederick P. Kenkel at the top of a list of the few American Catholics who pioneered social reform and labor legislation before World War I—along with men like Father Peter E. Dietz (one time coeditor of *Central-Blatt and Social Justice*), Fathers William J. Kerby, J. Elliot Ross, Frederick Siedenburg, S.J., Dr. David McCabe, and some others. Some of these were, of course, in close contact with one another. If one pages through the early volumes of the *Central-Blatt* (now *Social Justice Review*) one cannot but be amazed at the abundance of truly sound and solid essays on the social question published therein by men who soon moved into the forefront of American social Catholi-

95

cism, such as Fathers W. Engelen, S.J., Albert Muntsch, S.J., Joseph Husslein, S.J., Charles P. Bruehl, J. Elliot Ross, C.S.P., and such laymen as Frank O'Hara, David Goldstein, Louis F. Budenz. If these men did not write, they were busy preaching the gospel of social justice from their pulpits and their academic chairs, or teaching in social institutes sponsored by the Central Bureau of the Central Verein, the country's oldest federation of Catholic organizations (founded in Baltimore in 1855) and "the American heir to the spirit of Windthorst and Ketteler."[213]

Kenkel and Ryan

Albert Franz, who wrote the first history of social Catholicism in Germany up to the time of the death of Ketteler, called attention to the fact that Ketteler did not believe in governmental protection of labor as a permanent function of the state but regarded it as a temporary or provisional measure.[214] Eventually, these functions should be turned over to status corporations, that is, to autonomous bodies of people engaged in the same social and economic function. It is important to note that Kenkel, the *spiritus rector* of the Central Verein, followed exactly in Ketteler's footsteps, being opposed from the first to the extension of Federal power, exemplified later in his rejection of the Child Labor Amendment and of what he considered the state socialism of the New Deal.[215] Kenkel was indeed, as Albert Muntsch once expressed it, "a man after the heart of Ozanam and Ketteler."[216]

Ryan relates that the first time he read *Rerum novarum* he was most impressed by the passage in Section 28 (cf. *supra*, p. 82).[217] Actually this passage is a clear statement of the principle of subsidiarity, but at that time Ryan seems to have been fascinated by the pope's acceptance of state intervention and overlooked the important qualifications made by Leo. As we shall see later, Ryan all through his life felt that what governments normally do, and what appears to be practically necessary, may be regarded as belonging to the proper functions of government—a rather pragmatic point of view, quite similar to that of Hitze in Germany.

There can, thus, be no doubt that these foremost representatives of social Catholicism, Kenkel and Ryan, differed as regards the function of government in social and economic matters

—a situation not unlike that in many other countries, where Catholic leaders, of one mind as to the need for social reform, disagree concerning the ways and means of achiêving this end. This difference is not merely a matter of temperament, or a matter of the degree of intervention. In other words, we are here confronted with a difference which is not exclusively one of prudential judgment but also one of principle, depending on one's view of the nature and functions of government.

There was, however, much that these men (and their respective followers) had in common, particularly the rejection of the principle of *laissez faire*, of uncontrolled economic liberty, so typical for the kind of capitalism that prevailed in the nineteenth century, which has been said to have lasted, not from such arbitrary dates as 1800 to 1900, but from 1789 to World War I.

LATE CAPITALISM AND CATHOLICISM

World War I Spawns Collectivism

World War I was the spawning ground of economic and social collectivism. It was probably the first war in human history which displayed such a propensity for all-inclusiveness. While not itself a truly total war, it may be looked upon as a prologue to it. In its ruins, Bolshevism was born. From its battlefields there rose the future leaders of Fascism and National Socialism, Mussolini and Hitler.

In an essay long forgotten but more timely today than some 45 years ago, when it was written, the philosopher, Max Scheler, gave the first inkling of the concept of total war. His essay compares militarism of the mind (*Gesinnungsmilitarismus*) and pragmatical militarism (*Zweckmilitarismus*).[218] By the first type, Scheler meant the "militarism" of the professional soldier and of the standing army as distinguished from the civilian frame of mind. By pragmatical militarism he meant the newer technological or utilitarian concept of military action more typical of the defense systems and the warfare of democratic nations. We are here not interested in Scheler's at first somewhat startling proposition that professional militarism, characterized by a high regard for honor and chivalry, is much less warlike and cruel than the dehumanized,

97

scientific type of what might be called the engineering militarism of modern, supposedly peaceloving, democracies. It is the latter type which pits nation against nation and reduces the military to a technical tool of civilian governments.

Modern war, which aims at reducing personal physical risk and prefers efficiency (of destruction) to bravery, has probably had a great share in the transformation of full capitalism into late capitalism. No attempt will be made to give an adequate account of the third stage of capitalism which, as we shall see, represents a dialectic return to its origins: Mercantilism or controlled economy. Mars stood godfather to mercantilism; Mars returned to act as sponsor to late capitalism or neomercantilism.

The Waning of Capitalism

What are the characteristic features of that which, according to Sombart, is the final stage of capitalism? Here is an outline which closely follows Sombart's own, but brings it up to date: Rapidly spreading industrialization, now reaching and entering the underdeveloped regions of the world.[219] In all important phases of the economy, individual proprietorship disappears and is replaced by the corporation, the *société anonyme*. Corporate management, in contradistinction to individual entrepreneurship, is no longer guided by the intuitive, speculative, and daring impulses which motivated yesterday's businessman. In other words, rationalism takes the place of the irrational traits in the entrepreneur of the competitive phase of capitalism. Science now permeates all branches of business administration: production, personnel relations, and marketing. As far as possible, nothing is left to chance. The functions of the capitalistic enterpriser have been taken over by specialists: the accountant, the market analyst, the personnel manager, and so on. Management strives for growth rather than for profit or, more correctly, for optimal reinvestment of profits, rather than for a rise in distributable profit, i.e., in dividends. Growth leads to bigness, big businesses tend to merge, merged business tends to become bureaucratic. Business decisions are increasingly submitted to trade associations, cartels, and similar organizations. The purpose of these organizations is, as a rule, the restraint of trade. There is a tendency toward "mixed" public-private and cooperative enterprises and governmental corporations, as well as increasing government regulation of private business. To the increase in combinational and governmental control of business, there corresponds a decrease in private initiative, owner-control of business, and competition. The restraint of trade, that is, of economic freedom is partly self-imposed, partly government imposed, partly enforced by labor. Labor-management relations become increasingly impersonal and technical, with the union tending to become "part of the control system of management" (Daniel Bell). Rapid mechanization and, more recently, automation is causing a shift in the composition of the labor force, moving an ever-increasing number of workers from agriculture and manufacturing into the service industries— or into the ranks of the unemployed. Governments have taken it upon themselves to use monetary and fiscal measures, especially deficit-financing, to fill the gap between total output and private effective demand and thus to alleviate serious unemployment. It remains to be seen whether such antidepression measures will solve the problem of full employment in the long run. But it is evident that government moderation of economic fluctuation is turning governments into a dominant factor in their respective economies. Through tax-supported social security measures, the working classes are rapidly deproletarianized: they no longer depend entirely on the "sale" of their labor power to subsist. Working-class-consciousness subsides with the rise of living standards and the movement of workers into the middle classes. But with technological unemployment increasing and tending to become permanent, new social problems arise: the problem of what W. H. Ferry calls the "liberated margin" (the technologically displaced), the problem of leisure, of accelerated superannuation and early retirement, of income redistribution to sustain consumer demand, of social costs, and numerous other problems. These problems seem to have one thing in common: they must be solved to avoid disaster, but they cannot be solved singlehandedly by the process of competition between individual firms, nor simply by the process of "countervailing power." Ever since the end of World War I and the rapid growth of industrial and business combinations, labor unions, and other special-interest groups, a gradual change in the concept and in the actual functions of the state is taking place. At times, the state is clearly the mouthpiece and tool of these pluralistic forces, at other times and in other places the state sustains or recaptures its role as guardian and trustee of public welfare.

World War I and the End of Laissez Faire

To understand this development, it is necessary to return once more to our historical starting point, World War I. In all nations actively participating in that war, it was soon felt necessary to "mobilize" and "regiment" the economy. *Laissez faire*, which had started to break down during the latter part of the nineteenth century, crumbled under the impact of wartime controls. Free international trade was probably the first to vanish from the historical scene. With rapidly developing shortages in almost all lines of business, domestic competition, too, shrank and all but disappeared. The war economy of all or most belligerents included profit, wage and price-controls, rationing of civilian supplies, and the speed-up of production. To husband scarce manpower, the movement toward rationalization (stressing mechanization and efficiency) and standardization, which had already been in evidence before the war, was now accentuated and accelerated.[220] Not only the methods of production changed, but the products also. In our own day of much more rapid technological progress it is difficult to recognize and appreciate the impetus which World War I gave to the perfection of automotive vehicles and the airplane, to the advancements in the chemistry of synthetics, and even to the progress of the electronics industry. Mass production suggested the integration of productive processes in related industries and eventually the amalgamation and concentration of the producing firms themselves.[221] While in the prewar combinations (cartels, trusts) the constituent firms were still legally and managerially separate, there was now a tendency in the direction of centralized managerial control.

Walter Rathenau, Symbol of the Great Change

It is significant that the German industrialist who at the beginning of World War I had urged his government to institute government controls of the economy and was then himself appointed czar of the German war economy, Walter Rathenau, soon after the war proposed a type of cartel corporatism to restore Germany's depleted economic strength. Rathenau was president of Germany's biggest electric concern, the A.E.G., later secretary of foreign affairs of the new German Republic, and as a Jew was assassinated in 1922 by members of a terrorist gang of extreme nationalists. An exceedingly successful industrialist and a true statesman, imbued with a high sense of responsibility for national welfare, his plan of a "compulsory grouping of all German industry in an integrated system of semi-public, self-governing cartels"[222] could not be rejected as the mere chimera of an intellectual romanticist. He felt that Germany's collapse in 1918 gave her a unique opportunity to rebuild her economy along lines which would give greater emphasis to social welfare and would bring about the nonviolent emancipation of the proletariat. His own experiences with private enterprise during the 1914 mobilization had convinced Rathenau that *laissez faire* had played out its historical role and that uncontrolled competition could no longer adequately serve the ultimate purpose of the economy, namely the welfare of the national community as a whole. The corporations and combinations, he felt, must be made to serve the national economy by integrating them into an organic system of vocational and industrial corporations, operating through functional representation. The war economy which he had organized in 1914, based on an integrated structure of semipublic concerns (war cartels), could have served as a practical starting point.

Postwar German Corporatism and Father Pesch

Rathenau found a greater echo among Catholics than among the moderate socialists then in power or among his fellow industrialists. Heinrich Pesch, S.J., distinguished economist and architect of "solidarism" in the fourth volume of his textbook on economics, reprinted a long passage from Rathenau's book *In Days to Come* (Berlin: 1917; London: 1921) in which the latter draws attention to the serious harm resulting from a "disorganized, unregulated, unrestrained" system of free enterprise, and the urgent need for a regulation of the process of production.[223] At that time (1917), Rathenau still believed in far-reaching government intervention, while Pesch expected the economic order of tomor-

101

row to be one based predominantly on vocational groups (industry councils). By 1922, when Pesch quoted Rathenau's wartime
book, Rathenau had actually come very close to Pesch's point of
view. Father Pesch, following the Aristotelian–scholastic principle
of the proper mean, which is primarily a metaphysical and only
secondarily an ethical principle, always stressed that for a Christian the solution can be only one which is equally far removed
from the unrealistic concepts of individualism and socialism. These
social philosophies are unrealistic because they are not in keeping
with the being of man as a person and with his social nature.
Solidarism is not to be looked upon as an ethical ideal added
to or superimposed upon society. It is, rather, the true mode of
being of society, demonstrating the creative polarity of the (ontological) personality and sociality of man. Social life must build
on, and respect, the being of man as a person, an individual of a
rational nature that is master of its own acts. A true society cannot but consist of persons, free to act, true images of their divine
maker. Vice versa, it is in association, in the practice of the social virtues, that the human person thrives and achieves perfection. Solidarity, thus, boils down to the old adage: "All for each
and each for all."[224] Without such mutuality society is not
merely "bad" but deficient of being, i.e., nonexistent. With it,
it develops into a moral organism in which each part contributes
to the welfare of the whole without losing its identity. As an integrating force, solidarity will also effect the corporate coordination of the many functioning component parts and members of
economic society. It is on this sociophilosophic basis that Pesch
postulated a functional organization of the economy. Richard
E. Mulcahy, S.J., one of America's foremost students of Peschian
economic philosophy, has demonstrated convincingly that Pesch
considered the arrangement of economic society in interdependent
parts, each having a special function with respect to the whole, a
perennial need, something without which no civil society can
reach perfection.[225] Pesch did not consider it the task of the social philosopher and economist, that is, his job, to produce a detailed blueprint of a corporate order, which would necessarily vary
according to the differing circumstances of time and place. It was,
he felt, up to the statesman to determine which particular type
would be most appropriate hic et nunc.

Franz Hitze and Corporatism

Franz Hitze was such a statesman.[226] A legislator for some four decades, he was keenly interested in the plans for a corporate economy developed by men like Walter Rathenau, Wichard G. von Möllendorf, and Rudolf Wissel. In his earlier years, Hitze had himself developed a program for corporative reconstruction. His book *Kapital und Arbeit* (Paderborn: 1880)—written when he was only 25 years old—proposed a type of guild socialism, though rather different from that later developed by Penty, Hobson, and Cole. But as a parliamentarian he became a meliorist, dedicated to immediate betterment of the conditions of the working classes, laying aside his program of comprehensive social reform until a more appropriate time. After the war that time seemed to have arrived. In what he called an "epilogue" (*Nachwort*) to his early work on capital and labor, Hitze expressed satisfaction about the law of the new German Republic establishing shop stewards and work councils and the creation of a National Economic Council, which he felt represented a realization of some of his earliest ideas and ideals. In the Rathenau-Möllendorf outline of a corporative planned economy he found much that seemed to agree with his own hopes and beliefs, though it also contained proposals which he considered unacceptable, especially the notion of a system of autonomous, semipublic cartels. "Cartel legislation," he wrote, "would be—more or less—a form of police supervision though not by policemen but by a board of experts . . . More important, however, and made urgently imperative by the prevailing distressed economic conditions, seems to be liquidation, or at least the improvement of the cartels, or their being supplemented by public-legal self-governing bodies of the industry," which would regulate production, attend to certain phases of the protection of the workers from the dangers of unemployment, and of the administration of labor law.[227]

Ryan's Postwar Meliorism

If statesmen in Germany were impressed with the performance of their war economic agencies, so were United States legislators and civil leaders with that of their own wartime agencies. John A. Ryan, for one, was intrigued especially by the effective operation of the War Labor Board and of the U. S. Employment Service.[228] While it convinced him of what can be achieved without the force of law and without compulsion, it also confirmed his belief in the positive role of government in social matters in general and labor problems in particular. Immediately after the end of hostilities Father Ryan drafted a program of social reconstruction which, though originally meant to be presented as an address to the Knights of Columbus in Louisville, was adopted by the episcopal executive committee of the National Catholic War Council and published in February, 1919, as the council's own program. As Father Gearty has pointed out, the program was not entirely new, but incorporated many of the legislative proposals which Ryan had made for over a decade. His articles in the *Catholic World* (July-August, 1909) on the subject were republished in 1919 by the Paulist Fathers, "revised to date," under a title which very appropriately characterizes Ryan's approach to the social question: "A Program of Social Reform by Legislation."[229] Ryan started out with the question whether the then prevailing trend toward wider state intervention should be permitted to continue until it has embraced the full program of socialism or whether it should be countered by, and confined to, a program which will keep it within the bounds of feasible and rational social reform. He felt that the majority of Americans, if confronted with this alternative, would opt in favor of the latter proposition. He then proceeded to outline such a program which should aim at "regulating the limits, both upper and lower, of industrial opportunity," by securing to the laborers a reasonable minimum of wages and other economic goods, and by preventing monopoly capital from enriching itself at the expense of the consumer.

Ryan's Legislative Program

It is very significant that now social action is no longer aimed primarily at eliminating *laissez faire* and restraining competition but at restraining monopolistic tendencies. This reflects the change from full to late capitalism. It is in keeping with this historical turn that Ryan calls for competition which—outside the field of natural monopoly—should dominate industry, though the practice of it should be neither unrestricted nor debasing. Ryan felicitously calls it: maximization of actual opportunity for all (p. 5). In addition to minimum wage laws to assure all workers a decent livelihood, there should be maximum hour laws, to increase the leisure and improve the health of laborers, and laws providing for conciliation and arbitration, even, as the *ultima ratio*, compulsory arbitration. The problem of unemployment should be met by state employment bureaus, unemployment insurance, and —surprisingly—"state labor colonies," that is, it seems, labor camps, which he thought "could be of great benefit to certain classes of the unemployed" (p. 14). In addition to unemployment insurance, there should be social insurance legislation covering sickness, occupational diseases, industrial accidents, and old age. Municipalities should be made to remove the slums and provide decent housing for people of moderate or small means. But not only the working classes should be protected but also the whole body of consumers. Ryan hoped to achieve this by means which match his suggestion of labor camps, namely, by gradual nationalization of railroads, power companies, water works, municipal transportation, and telephones. He believed that the most decisive answer to possible objections "is the fact that the policy of public ownership is gaining ground every day in every country, and that no country now enjoying it has any thought of reverting to the other system" (p. 17), an answer which strikes one as rather pragmatic reasoning. Ryan would turn big steel and oil companies, and any other firm whose large size seems to be justified by the economies of scale (or of mass production) into public utilities just like some of the natural monopolies. However, if the socialist prediction of the inevitable concentration and monopolization in all industries should prove correct and state regulation of prices ineffective, then outright government ownership of artificial monopolies should be tried. Where Ryan proposes higher inheritance taxes, he suggests that the additional revenues derived from it be used for public work projects and for financing social "insurance." As in tax-financing of social insurance, Ryan comes close to Bismarck's concept of insurance-like benefits for the working classes, and he comes close to Henry George's ideas when he proposes the taxing away of "unearned increments" in the value of land. Unearned incomes through stock and commodity exchange manipulations should also be prevented by law. Ryan anticipated the accusation that his program was socialistic or paternalistic, but this, he felt would be an attempt at refutation by name-calling, not deserving serious attention.

The "Bishops' Program"

Not a few of these proposals can indeed be found again in the Program of Social Reconstruction of the Administrative Committee of the National Catholic War Council, of February 12, 1919.[230] The so-called bishops' program, however, endeavors also and first of all to answer the special problems that had arisen with the war, the end of hostilities, and the return of large numbers of war veterans. The pronouncement by the Bishops Muldoon, Hayes, Schrembs, and Russel first reviews the program offered by the British Labor Party, the A. F. of L., by American and British employers, and the Interdenominational Conference of Social Service Unions, and then proceeds to formulate its own scheme. At the outset, the bishops say—in Ryan's words—that they will make no attempt to propose a comprehensive program, because on the one hand no profound changes are to be expected in postwar American society, and on the other, because such a program would not only meet with little response but would also seriously interfere with solving those problems which demand immediate attention, namely the social problems of demobilization, especially relocation and readjustment of the discharged soldiers. The bishops urged that the U.S. Employment Service and the National War Labor Board, which both functioned successfully during the war, be continued, that special care be taken in the relocation of women war workers, that the then prevailing wage rates be sustained, that the municipalities take over from the Federal government the work of providing adequate housing for workers and that wartime price controls, instead of merely being abolished, be replaced by measures which would effectively eliminate monopolistic price fixing. Happily, not only legislative and administrative measures to reduce the cost of living were proposed but also "private" ones, such as the formation of consumer cooperatives and the training of the people generally in the habit of saving.

106

Corporatist Implications

The program then turns from the agencies and laws that have been put in operation during the war to peacetime labor legislation and such problems as social insurance, labor participation in management, vocational training, and child labor. It should be noted, however, that in the section on social insurance it is stated that "any contribution to the insurance fund from the general revenues of the state should be only slight and temporary" (p. 254); ordinarily, the fund should be raised by a levy on industry, as was then done in the case of accident compensation. The following statement could have been lifted out of one of Franz Hitze's early works, or, for that matter, out of many a book written by European representatives of corporatism: "The industry in which a man is employed should provide him with all that is necessary to meet all the needs of his entire life" (*ibid.*).

It is hard to understand why neither Ryan nor the Catholic War Council realized, or so it seems, the "corporatist" implications of this statement. Perhaps it is really not so hard to understand if one recalls that, after all, America had known no Middle Ages. In all fairness, we cannot be expected to have an awareness of that organic and, in the best sense of the word, "pluralistic" social order, which existed—with all its shortcomings—in precapitalistic times. It is surprising enough that after *Quadragesimo anno* social Catholicism in the United States did develop an appreciation of this concept for which there did not exist in this country any historical precedents.[231] This is not to say that the idea of functional representation, as developed in the encyclical, *Quadragesimo anno*, is a medieval one or that Pius XI's "industries and professions" represent a revival of the guild system. It is merely to point out that the historical continuity with the Middle Ages and the many reminders and witnesses of the past ages which surrounded him, may make it easier for the European to have an "empathetic" understanding for the idea of a social order built on autonomous industries and vocations.

The program also called for labor participation in management. Even though reference is made to shop committees it seems that what is suggested goes beyond the traditional concept of "industrial democracy." In recommending that labor gradually be given greater representation in the "industrial" part of management (including control of processes, machinery, nature of product) the program comes close to what nowadays is called "codetermination."

Ultimate Aims?

Toward the end of the program it is stated that a reflection on ultimate aims cannot be entirely neglected. The reasons given for at least a brief discussion of comprehensive and fundamental reforms are somewhat unusual: because other groups are busy issuing such systematic pronouncements and because it satisfies our desire for statements of this kind. The need for something of the kind of a philosophical foundation is admitted, but it sounds almost as if it is largely in order to please people who enjoy generalities. Actually in the subsequent review of the main defects of the prevailing system, the deficiences listed are all of a practical rather than of a sociophilosophical nature. In lieu of an inquiry into ultimate ends and comprehensive reforms, the program closes with the admonition that all legal and institutional changes would be in vain without a new spirit, without a return to Christian principles (cf. p. 259).

The Central Verein and the "Bishops' Program"

It is interesting to note that the Central Verein and its organ, the *Central-Blatt*, that had always given special attention to basic principles, praised the program for its many practical suggestions. Father Bruehl, surprisingly, even considered them somewhat tame (zahm), but then asked the question, whether all these "reconstruction" proposals are not really aiming at repair, merely mending rather than reconstructing. Bruehl felt that there was in the program an overemphasis on industrial labor problems, resulting in (or being the result of) a neglect of the over-all social question. Bruehl warned particularly against any attempt to copy the German social insurance system, which he thought was by no means worthy of imitation. He expressed doubts that the views of the Administrative Committee of the National Catholic War Council were really the views of the American hierarchy; he was sure that one could not claim that they represented the teachings of the universal Church.[232] There are no indications that at that time it was known that the "Program" was actually the work of John A. Ryan. At times it seems that the leaders of the Central Verein suspected it. Father W. E. Engelen, for one, expressed concern about Ryan's practicalism.[233]

The "Program" and the "Pastoral"

One should think that if the bishops of the United States had simply identified themselves with the program, they would have had little reason to include in their Pastoral Letter, issued only seven months later, a special section on industrial relations.[234] This pastoral letter of the American hierarchy, however, was signed by Cardinal Gibbons, their quasi-primate, whom we may rightly assume to have been quite sympathetic with Ryan's program. It is also worthy of note that twenty years later, in 1939, the bishops' program was republished by the National Catholic Welfare Conference with a preface by Archbishop (later Cardinal) Mooney of Detroit, at that time chairman of the Administrative Board of the N.C.W.C. These two facts seem to favor the assumption that the board's program was really the bishops' program, particularly if one keeps in mind that, after all, the episcopal board was appointed by the hierarchy of the United States. Be that as it may, the "tenor" of the industrial relations section of the pastoral letter of 1919 does differ from that of the program, which latter was nowhere in the pastoral even as much as mentioned. This section represents a somewhat belated joint endorsement of Rerum novarum, more balanced, one should say, than the program and making it a point that the social question is not merely an economic but also and primarily a moral and religious matter. It was as if the bishops wish to drive home a point where and when they stress the fact that management and labor have disregarded the claim of the people as a whole which is prior to their own. Instead of reconfirming the right to strike, the bishops forcefully point out the limits of the strike as a weapon used in the industrial conflict. Instead of making a point of and dwelling upon that conflict, the bishops stress the fact that basically the conflicting parties belong together and have common interests. To the unquestioned right of labor to organize there corresponds the equally indisputable right of employers to the faithful observance by the labor unions of their contracts and agreements. Where agreements are unobtainable through negotiations, disputes should always be submitted to arbitration instead of letting economic power decide the issue.

The Pastoral Anticipates Vocational Group Order

In its final section on the benefit of association, the pastoral letter does what the Catholic War Council's Program failed to do: It proposes joint labor-management boards or associations, not to supplant but supplement the labor market organizations. The fact that Cardinal Gibbons, who almost three decades before was probably instrumental in a revision of the final draft of *Rerum novarum* to the effect that the encyclical recognized unions, in addition to mixed organizations of employers and employees, now signed a letter which stressed the need for such mixed organizations to supplement the unions cannot be overestimated. Actually it was but a shift of emphasis but a significant one. Instead of calling for operative councils and codetermination, which tend to invade property rights, the pastoral letter says that the time has come for "associations and conferences, composed jointly of employers and employees, which will place emphasis upon the common interests rather than the divergent aims of the two parties, upon cooperation rather than conflict." The worker is indeed to "participate in those matters of industrial management which directly concern him and about which he possesses helpful knowledge," which, it is hoped, will increase his sense of personal dignity and responsibility, his interest and pride in what he is doing, his efficiency and contentment. This kind of comanagement, if we may use this term, is not aggressive or demanding but cooperative, though not surrendering any natural and vested rights. The bishops refer to the Middle Ages, stating that though its economic institutions cannot be restored, its spirit is of permanent application and "the only one that will give stability to industrial society."[235]

"The Bishops Take Command"

Looking backward, the bishops' pastoral letter of 1919 strikes one as a harbinger of a social Catholic spring in America. It was the first pastoral since 1884 and its broad outlook and verve bespoke a spirit of determination and action. Aaron Abell has given

110

us a comprehensive and practically complete picture of the era of reconstruction that followed in the wake of World War I. It need not be retold here. Abell aptly identified the new aspects of the historical situation by stating that now "the Bishops [took] command."[236] It will be remembered that in the past some bishops had taken a lively interest in social problems and aired their views in speeches, articles, and books. But it could not escape the attention of the more alert laity that even their spiritual leaders often differed considerably in their opinions about social and economic issues. Perhaps unaware of the relative freedom of Catholics—high and low—in matters of prudential judgment, the faithful were likely to be somewhat puzzled and helpless. The bishops now recognized that in this postwar era of political and social upheaval it was more than ever necessary for them to speak with one voice. They decided to meet annually, to address the faithful more regularly, and to transform the National Catholic War Council into a permanent listening post and mouthpiece of the hierarchy: the National Catholic Welfare Council (later "Conference"), which was to concentrate on educational and social matters. Bishop Peter J. Muldoon was commissioned to set up a Social Action Department. A group of priests and laymen that counseled the bishop, chose an executive committee among whose members we find such well-known Catholic social leaders as Fathers W. J. Kerby, Frederick Siedenburg, S.J., and Edwin V. O'Hara (later Archbishop) and Messrs. James E. Hagerty and Frederick P. Kenkel. Father (later Msgr.) John A. Ryan was appointed director of the department with Father Raymond A. McGowan as his assistant, thus assuring what Professor Abell called the "socially liberal influence" of the department.[237]

The Bishops Warn of Paternalism

While the Social Action Department sponsored badly-needed social legislation, the bishops made it clear that they were well aware of the dangers of paternalism in government and of the limits of government intervention. In February, 1922—a decade before the birth of the New Deal!—the Administrative Committee of the N.C.W.C. issued a statement which is well worth recalling and even seems more timely today than it was forty years ago. It reads as follows:

The growth of bureaucracy in the United States is one of the most significant aftereffects of the war. This growth must be resolutely checked. Federal assistance and federal direction are in some cases beneficial and even necessary, but extreme bureaucracy is foreign to everything American. It is unconstitutional and undemocratic. It means officialdom, red tape, and prodigal waste of public money. It spells hordes of so-called experts and self-perpetuating cliques of politicians to regulate every detail of daily life. It would eventually sovietize our form of government.

The forward-looking in our national life must resolutely stand against further encroachments on individual and state liberty. The press, the home, the school, and the Church have no greater enemy at the present time than the paternalistic and bureaucratic government which certain self-seeking elements are attempting to foist upon us.[238]

Wealth Concentration, Depression, and the Hierarchy

However, when the Great Depression hit this country, the bishops of the United States were among the first to stand up for the rights of the workmen in general and of the unemployed in particular.[239] Again we hear the voice of the hierarchy raised not only against those who object to any restriction of competition but also and even more against the "economic dictatorship" of those who desire restriction of competition not for the sake of national welfare but for selfish reasons: "Industry in our country through the concentration of wealth, has acquired such complete control that independent operation, even on the part of so-called [!] owners and employers, is practically impossible" (p. 276). Even in their discussion of the farm problem the bishops drew attention to the fact "that the concentration of wealth in the hands of the few has all but crushed agriculture, and has so drained the farm that the farmer finds it increasingly difficult to wrest a decent living from the land . . ." (p. 283). In the chapter on unemployment the bishops said that in spite of the typical American spirit of self-reliance and thrift, "the wealth of the nation gradually flowed into the hands of the few. Capitalists and industrialists, driven by greed, monopolized the sources of wealth and gained control of the products and profits made possible by the progress of technological science, to their own enrichment and to the impoverish-

112

ment and enslavement of the masses" (pp. 283 f). Implicitly, the bishops endorsed unemployment insurance and old age pensions, but they said that the depression was "not the time to make actual provision" for them. "Employment is our first consideration, not insurance against unemployment or, old age" (pp. 284 f).

The bishops then stated that prior to all practical measures there should be a general realization of the fact that "there can be no hope for the restoration of human society without restoring Christ, without striving to accord to man the dignity that he, as God, conferred on every human being. This must be the starting point" (p. 285). But those who are aware of the fact that "the recognition of the authority of Christ is essential for the restoration not only of the moral but also of the economic order" (p. 286), will likewise acknowledge the urgent need for a study of those economic and social facts to which the moral force of that authority applies. There is no substitute for the expert knowledge both of the fundamental principles and the realities of economic life, especially in the needed defense against hostile legislation which disregards human dignity and man's essential freedoms (pp. 288 f). In discussing the rights of the workingman—such as his right to a wage sufficient to sustain himself and his family in decent comfort, his right to organize, his right to share in the prosperity of business, and so on—the bishops particularly stress his right to ownership of productive property. But they warn against certain types of profit sharing and employee stock ownership where employees labor under the disadvantage of being minority stockholders. Labor should not envy management its legitimate profits nor should management deny labor its legitimate claim to a share in the affluence of society. The bishops fully recognized that the prosperity of big business is not always and necessarily the result of artificial monopolies but that of the so-called economies of scale. But it must be supervised and prevented from abusing its favorable position and the law must protect the smaller businesses from unfair encroachments by big corporations.

Corporatism vs. State Socialism

Toward the end, the bishops of the United States once more warn against the undiminished "tendency to place too much reliance on government to accomplish our economic salvation . . .

113

One of the greatest dangers facing us is a blind reaction from our former individualism to a regime of State socialism or State capitalism" (p. 292). That is why they, in keeping with the principle of subsidiarity, propose the "organization of the various economic groups along the lines of their separate industries and fields of endeavor" providing representation of every function in the economic group (p. 292).

In promoting what has been variously called the industy council plan, a vocational group order, a system of functional representation, or simply corporatism, the bishops followed, of course, the teachings of the (then) recent encyclical, *Quadragesimo anno*. If one were to express briefly what distinguished Pope Pius XI's encyclical *On Reconstructing the Social Order* from Leo XIII's *Rerum novarum*, one might say that it is the issue of totalitarianism and collectivism. *Rerum novarum*, written during the heyday of liberal capitalism, called upon the organizations of labor and especially upon the governments to protect laboring man from the furies of the unfettered forces of competition. *Laissez faire* was rampant and the workers' very life, health, and dignity was at stake. There could be no question yet of a comprehensive reorganization of the socioeconomic order.

The Search for a Better Economic Order

The Great War, as will be remembered, had changed the picture. Largely, though by no means exclusively, as a consequence of the destructions wrought by the war, of impoverishment, inflation, and, finally, after a few years of what has been called a "false prosperity," the Great Depression, government intervention had gained rapidly in dimension and intensity. Alongside and in competition with, the rising tide of governmentalism there developed the giants of business, ready to crush between them the very society which not so long ago seemed to have been delivered from the onslaughts of the competitive juggernaut. Now even so realistic an economist as John Maynard Keynes—years before he became a "Keynesian"—acknowledged "the end of the laissez faire" and the need to contemplate "the future organization of society."[240] Five years before *Quadragesimo anno* Keynes wrote: "I believe that in many cases the ideal size for the unit of control and organization lies somewhere between the individual and the modern

114

state. I suggest, therefore, that progress lies in the growth and the recognition of semi-autonomous bodies within the State—bodies whose criterion of action within their own fields is solely the public good as they understand it, and from whose deliberations motives of private advantage are excluded, though some place it may still be necessary to leave, until the ambit of men's altruism grows wider, to the separate advantage of particular groups, classes, or faculties—bodies which in the ordinary course of affairs are mainly autonomous within their prescribed limitations, but are subject in the last resort to the sovereignty of the democracy expressed through Parliament." He proposes, he said, in so many words, "a return—towards mediaeval conceptions of separate autonomies." He reminds his readers that "in England at any rate, corporations are a mode of government which has never ceased to be important and is sympathetic to our institutions." He believes that even in the United States—perhaps because of its Anglo-Saxon Law—"there are analogous instances."[241] Seven years before Berle and Means published their *The Modern Corporation and Private Property*, Keynes stated that corporate business enterprises, when they reach a certain age and size, approximate to the status of public corporations rather than to that of individualistic private enterprises. "One of the most interesting and unnoticed developments of recent decades has been the tendency of big enterprise to socialize itself. A point arrives in the growth of a big institution . . . at which the owners of the capital, i.e., the shareholders, are almost entirely dissociated from the management, with the result that the direct personal interest of the latter in the making of great profit becomes quite secondary."[242] The result, Keynes believed, is "a waning of enterprise" and a trend in the direction of state socialism. "We must take full advantage of the natural tendencies of the day, and we must probably prefer semi-autonomous corporations to organs of the Central Government . . ."[243]

Keynes' expositions should convince even the most skeptical student of social Catholicism that the idea of a corporate reorganization of society was and is not a "pipe dream" of Catholic medievalists. The late Harvard economist Joseph Schumpeter wrote that "a reorganization of society on the lines of the encyclical *Quadragesimo anno* . . . no doubt provides an alternative to socialism that would avoid the 'omnipotent state.' "[244] Werner

115

Sombart, another non-Catholic economist, did not hesitate to quote several passages from *Quadragesimo anno* in Latin, calling it an encyclical of "unheard of beauty" (*unerhört schöne*).[245]

European Antecedents of Quadragesimo Anno

It should interest the reader that friends, colleagues, and stu-dents of Sombart belonged to that Study Circle of Königswinter on the Rhine which did the pioneer work for the encyclical, as similar study circles did such work for *Rerum novarum*. This Königswinter round-table conference consisted of the following Catholic economists and sociologists: Dr. Theodor Brauer of the University of Cologne, Dr. Goetz Briefs, professor at the Berlin Institute of Technology, Father Gustav Gundlach, S.J., successor to the late Heinrich Pesch, S.J., Dr. Paul Jostock at the Federal Institute for Business Cycle Analysis, Berlin, Father Rudolf Kai-bach, O.M. Cap. of the Capuchin seminary of Krefeld, Dr. Franz H. Mueller of the Institute of Social Research at the University of Cologne, Oswald von Nell-Breuning, S.J., professor at the graduate school of philosophy and theology, Frankfurt on the Main, Dr. Heinrich Rommen, Director of the Social Action De-partment of the Catholic People's Union, München-Gladbach, Father Wilhelm Schwer, professor of Catholic social theory at the University of Bonn. These men met from time to time at the Workers' College of the Christian Trade Unions in the town of Königswinter at the foot of the Siebengebirge, to discuss the social question and the role of the Church in the area of social reform. Msgr. Joseph van der Velden, later bishop of Aachen, at that time head of the Volksverein (People's Union), and his assistant Dr. Rommen were the organizers and instigators of these meet-ings. The Volksverein had for many years been Msgr. Hitze's domain of educational activity and the spirit of its Social Action Department was very much like that of the Social Action Depart-ment of the N.C.W.C. under Msgr. Ryan and his successors. The meetings of the Königswinter council, however, were meant to lead beyond the confines of legislative social policy toward a more com-prehensive social reform. Practically all participants were solidar-ists, who recognized with Heinrich Pesch, S.J., who only a few years earlier had died, the need for social legislation, as well as—

116

now more than ever—for a fundamental reorganization of the social economy along corporate lines. The Volksverein organized supplemental social weeks, such as France had had since 1904, in order to carry the fruits of the Königswinter deliberations to a wider public.[246] In Vienna met a study circle of Catholic sociologists most of whom were not sociologists, in the technical sense of the word, but social Catholics of the Vogelsang school, ardent antisolidarists and anticapitalists. The group eventually published a Manifesto, which was really a mere syllabus of social concepts, reducing capitalism to an "usurious economic system." As Alfred Diamant has rightly pointed out the manifesto, because it was a compromise, pleased no one. "It was too radical for the moderates and the hierarchy, and not radical enough for the Vogelsang disciples."[247]

Of all the study circles and conferences meeting in the late 20s and early 30s, the one of Königswinter gained a certain prominence as one of its members, Father von Nell, S.J., was eventually called to Rome, apparently to assist with the drafting of the encyclical, *Quadragesimo anno*.[248] It is generally recognized that this encyclical follows the solidarist middle road, confirming the teachings of Pesch. Father Gundlach was appointed professor at the Gregorian University in Rome and became advisor to Pope Pius XII.[249]

Totalitarianism and World War II

When Hitler seized power in Germany, the voice of social Catholicism in Germany, and soon afterward in Austria, was stilled. Nor was there any independent Catholic social movement in Italy, Spain, and Portugal. With the start of World War II public interest in other European countries, of necessity, turned to the war effort. In the countries invaded by Hitler's armies, Catholic social leaders, when not arrested, had to go into hiding or exile.

Perhaps the only nation in which the Catholic social movement —and a "movement" it now was—could continue to operate with almost undiminished vigor was the United States. Under the leadership of John A. Ryan social Catholicism in this country enjoyed during the depression something approaching official recognition. As Hitze in Germany before World War I, so Ryan rose, in a manner, to be the architect of social legislation in this country, enjoying the special confidence of President Franklin D. Roosevelt.

When Pius XI's encyclical, *On Reconstructing the Social Order,* was published, Ryan and his followers felt it to be a complete vindication of their own teachings and actions. Father Gearty says that Ryan was particularly pleased by the fact that *Quadragesimo anno* approved of or suggested a modification of the wage contract by a contract of partnership which would permit the workers to share in the ownership, and consequently also in the management and earnings of the firm in and for which they work. Another passage which appears to have delighted him was the one in which the Holy Father confirmed the view that "certain forms of property must be reserved to the state."[250] Ryan considered that there was much in the National Recovery Administration established in Roosevelt's New Deal administration that resembled the occupational group system, as outlined in *Quadragesimo anno.*[251] It would not be fair to give the impression that Ryan picked out a few passages of the encyclical that appealed to him and disregarded what he himself called "the most constructive and original part of the Encyclical," namely the part dealing with the reconstruction of the social order. He does call attention to the principle of subsidiarity and the vocational groups, although he does not particularly dwell and enlarge upon it.[252] Later, in an article, "Shall the NRA be Scrapped?," Ryan tells that when he first read the passages of the encyclical outlining the pope's plan for corporate reconstruction, he thought and "feared that its realization was a long, long way off, a thing to be piously hoped for rather than confidently expected."[253] The Central Verein did not seem to share John A. Ryan's optimistic interpretation of the N.R.A. as something capable of being developed into a corporate order. The emphasis of the encyclical was, they felt, on a reduction rather than an extension of government intervention. The planned economy, seemingly contemplated by the New Deal, was in their opinion anything but a realization of the pope's plan. State socialism would perpetuate rather than basically change the prevailing socioeconomic order.[254] Whatever one may think about the objection to the New Deal voiced by Frederick P. Kenkel, his erstwhile assistant Edward Koch, and others, there should be no doubt that it was not at all dictated by reactionary motives, but by a deep and sincere desire for a more profound change of the social order than the one provided by a simple extension of labor legislation and government intervention.

Once More: The Depression and the Church

Needless to say that in striving for a "better economic order," to use a phrase coined by John A. Ryan, American social Catholicism in general and the American hierarchy in particular did not lose sight of proximate social evils, such as "the destructive practices in finance, government, and business," which afflicted this country particularly in Depression days. Yet the bishops pointed out that in the final analysis, all these evils are crimes "against the Christian concept of society." This concept and all the Christian social principles, the bishops stated, should be speedily "made familiar to all the faithful," not forgetting the masses of those who suffered "under the present collapse of our social order."[255] Yet, while again stressing the inherent right of workers to organize in defense of their basic rights,[256] the bishops felt it necessary to remind labor of the fact that it has duties no less than management.

In November, 1937, the hierarchy of the United States, speaking through the archbishops and bishops of the Administrative Board of the National Catholic Welfare Conference, expressed anxiety about the increasing agitation of "cunning propagandists" who then tried to capitalize on widespread misery and discontent of the masses, preaching to them the gospel of class hatred. The bishops exposed in particular the left-wing intellectuals, especially professors and teachers, who claimed the constitutional right of freedom of utterance only to propagate and erect a new order which will deny that very liberty which they now abuse.[257] The Church can never identify herself with any system which rejects and destroys the natural rights of man and his civil liberties, not even with a system of "governmental bureaucracy" or "ubiquitous governmental control." Labor, the bishops said, should stay clear of such fallacious social philosophies and "not incur the charge of countenancing coercion and injustice." They did not hesitate to say, what nowadays in certain, even Catholic quarters, would be regarded as a sure sign of a reactionary mind, viz., that "there are many [!] honorable employers, whose motives are dictated by justice and charity."[258] These businessmen should be commended, the bishops declared, especially since business is increasingly developing in the direction of depersonalization and, therefore, of irresponsibility: "responsibility is . . . divorced from ownership" and control "is exercised by those who are not the real owners of wealth but merely the trustees and administrators of invested funds."[259] This type of control of management is undermining democracy and self-determination from within. But this is not all. "Another method of destroying the liberty of the people," the bishops went on to say, "although it begins by lauding democracy and proclaiming freedom, is to establish the dictatorship of an absolutist State," a kind of state which "is contrary to the letter and spirit of the American Constitution." "It first gives the people many services; and then it assumes a multiplicity of functions which no normal civil government should attempt to discharge." This inevitably leads to a slave state. But the people seem not to realize it, for "the tendency of our time is to make more and more demands on government." "Citizens and groups should not ask the government to do for them what they can do for themselves. Sound social policy requires government to encourage citizens to assume as much personal responsibility as possible. The poor and laboring classes should resist the tendency to set up the omnipotent State. Their chief economic defense is organization. The traditional and ideal Christian society is not an individualistic but an organic society in which the individual, through the instrumentality of his group, works for himself, his group, and the entire social body." The bishops expressed concern about the split, then taking place in the American Federation of Labor, leading to the formation of the Congress of Industrial Organizations. "It is essential that labor unions be governed by the principle of Christian brotherhood, justice and fair play. They should embrace all groups of workers. While seeking to promote their own interests they should be guided by sound judgment, have regard for the common economic good, respect property rights, prove themselves worthy of the confidence of every community, and thus perform their rightful function in protecting the legitimate interests of their members and in giving strength and stability to the nation."[260]

WORLD WAR II AND THE SOCIAL QUESTION

In the following year, a year marked by the international tension building up on account of the steady rise of Nazi power in Germany, the American episcopate reminded the faithful of the fact that the conflict between the nation had the same roots as the conflict between the classes of society: greed and selfishness. Against these, they said, there simply is no other remedy but love of God and neighbor. "To Catholic labor leaders and unionists, as well as to the Catholic employers, we express the profound hope that they will bend their best energies to the realization of the Christian social order envisaged by the Holy Father, to the end that, achieving first a true industrial and social peace at home, we may thus contribute to a lasting peace among all nations."[261]

Almost exactly a year later, Pope Pius XII took up the same problem, that of greed and selfishness spreading rapidly through the political realm in the form of absolute state autonomy, atheistic dictatorship, and totalitarianism: "The conception," the Holy Father said, "which assigns to the State unlimited authority is not only pernicious to the internal life of the nation, to its prosperity, and to the orderly increase of its well-being; it also damages relations between peoples, because it breaks the unity of international society, it rips out the foundations and the value of the rights of people . . ."[262] If the absolute state yet progresses, it is due to some extent to its apparent efficiency and prosperity: "It is certainly true that power based on such weak, precarious foundations may sometimes achieve, because of contingent circumstances, material success which astonishes the superficial observer; but there comes a moment when there triumphs that inescapable law which strikes everything that is built on a hidden or open disproportion between the greatness of material and outward success and the weakness of inner values and their moral foundations."[263]

What is true of the state and of government is true also of the social bodies within the state. They, too, are often as "successful" as they are powerful. On the occasion of the one hundred and fiftieth anniversary of the establishment of the ecclesiastical hierarchy in the United States, Pius XII, in his encyclical *Sertum laetitiae* of the Feast of All Saints, 1939, mentions the fact that even this prosperous country has not been entirely spared social conflict and interclass hostility: "You know full well," the Holy

Father said to the American bishops, "what aspect it [the social question] assumes in America, what acrimonies, what disorders it produces." Like the bishops themselves, so the pope stressed the natural right of all involved in this conflict, the producers and the laboring and farming classes, to join forces in order to "defend their proper rights and secure the betterment of the goods of soul and of body, as well as the honest comforts of life. But let the unions[264] in question draw their vital force from principles of wholesome liberty; let them take their form from the lofty rules of justice and of honesty, and, conforming themselves to those norms, let them act in such a manner that in their care for the interests of their class they violate no one's rights; let them continue to strive for harmony and respect the common weal of civil society."[265]

"Our Bishops Speak"

As if in response to this encyclical letter addressed to the Church in the United States, the Administrative Board and Assistant Bishops of the National Catholic Welfare Conference, on Ash Wednesday of the year 1940, issued a joint pastoral letter on the "Church and Social Order."[266] This letter may be looked upon as the most comprehensive statement of the American hierarchy on the social question. As did Pius XI in Quadragesimo anno, the bishops made it clear at the outset that the Church is concerned only with the moral aspects of that question and that she "does not prescribe any particular form of technical economic organization of society."[267] They then proceed to reiterate man's right to own private property, stressing, however, the individual and social aspect of ownership: "To deny the individual character and aspect of ownership leads to some form of socialism and collective ownership; to deny the social character or aspect of ownership leads to selfish individualism or that form of exaggerated liberalism which repudiates duties and ends in complete irresponsibility to other persons and to the common good." Again, as in November 1937, the bishops pointed out that the great dangers which society presently faces is the concentration of ownership and control of wealth as well as "its anonymous character which results from some of the existing business and corporation law, whereby responsibility toward society is greatly impaired if not completely ig-

122

nored."[268] It is the duty not only of the government, but also and primarily of the capital owners themselves and of management to work for a solution which would provide for an adjustment of ownership to meet the needs of social welfare. Due to wrong labor policies on the part of management and the fact that labor had no voice in the determination of policies affecting it, "in too many instances an undue portion of the income has been claimed by those who have ownership and control of capital, whilst those on the other hand who have only their labor to invest have been forced to accept working conditions which are unreasonable and wages which are unfair."[269] Labor can have no effective voice as long as it is not organized to bargain collectively. But bargaining too is subject to moral principles and not merely a matter of power. Principles that would hold that wages should provide for nothing more than the subsistence of the worker or that they should be determined solely by supply and demand, are both "anti-social and anti-Christian." These "principles" often serve merely to rationalize the ruthless use of power on the part of the employers. The bishops point out, however, "that the principle of force and domination is equally wrong if exercised by Labor under certain conditions by means of a monopoly control." "To defend the principle or to adopt in practice the theory that the net result belongs to labor and that capital should receive only sufficient to replace itself is an invasion of the rights of property. This is only a more subtle form of the contention that all means of production should be socialized. Clearly all such proposals disregard the contribution which the owner of property makes in the process of production and are palpably unjust."[270]

The Problems of Just Distribution

The immediate problem in labor relations in those days however, was not, the bishops declared, the excessive claims of labor on the income of industry but the abuse of power by both parties in the labor market. If employers fail to guard social justice, the human dignity of labor, neglecting the social nature of economic life and the interests of the common good, if employees engage in the criminal use of violence both against persons and property, the public authorities will have to step in to protect and defend rights and prevent disorder.

Among those rights, the rights of property are of special importance. This, however, does not mean merely the protection of lawful owners against unjust infringement upon their ownership, it also means protection and support of those who have been unjustly excluded from the lawful acquisition of property, those, the bishops say, "who constitute the proletariat or the propertyless."[271] It is the lack of sufficient private property and the exclusive dependence of the worker on a wage income, which leads to social insecurity and social disorder. An economic system "which tolerates such insecurity is both economically unsound and also inconsistent with the demands of social justice and social charity."[272] It is the responsibility of employers and employees to collaborate to effect a more equitable distribution of income and wealth between capital and labor, farmers and city dwellers, and even between the various trades and industrial groups of the workers themselves. Industry should not merely provide a living wage but also a saving wage which would provide for future emergencies. The bishops recognize that individual employers and industries cannot always achieve this end all by themselves, which may necessitate government support, financed through taxation.

This, the bishops declare, proves the truly vital importance of the problem of wages. While the wage contract is not intrinsically wrong, the exclusive dependence on a wage does, as was pointed out before, make for insecurity. Thus a modification of the wage contract which would give the worker a share in the capital ownership and in the profits of the company, would be in order. Such partnership in the firm would suggest a certain partnership in responsibility, a voice in management. However, the bishops leave no doubt that they do not mean "that labor should assume responsibility for the direction of business beyond its own competency and legitimate interest." Labor has no "right to demand dominating control over the distribution of profits. To set up such claims would amount to an infringement on the rights of property." But labor has real rights, such as the right, referred to before, to a wage which provides not only for subsistence but also for security, or the right to wage priority, according to which such a wage "constitutes the first charge on industry."[273] While employees should help their employer, if needs be, to weather difficulties beyond his control, the employer cannot rightfully expect his employees to subsidize his business by accepting unjust wages as a permanent arrangement. Neither can he expect them to share the burden of unfair competition to which he happens to be exposed. Such destructive competition must be fought through defensive organization and by legislative means. The bishops also plead for a certain stability of wages and prices which they demonstrate to be interdependent. "Rapid or frequent fluctuations disturb the harmonious proportions between income and prices not only for owners and employers but also for the workingmen themselves."[274] Workers should not lose sight of the fact that they are sometimes exploited by other workers whose unfair wage demands send prices up,[275] and that "some wage increases come *not* out of the profits of the wealthy but out of the increased prices for the poor."[276] In this connection, the bishops draw attention to what they call the "principle of interdependence," which refers not only to the relationship between ethics and economics, but also to the quasi organic character of economic society. He who violates the laws of justice and charity interferes simultaneously with the proper operation of the economy. Moreover, any such interference in one sector of the economy is likely to adversely affect other sectors, if not the economy as a whole.

The Establishment of Social Order

The bishops conclude their letter with a special chapter on the "establishment of social order." In it they warn against any merely pragmatic approach to the problem of a reorganization of social economy. This reorganization cannot be achieved, they say, by hastily passing laws or simply by new governmental policies. It calls in the first place for careful reflection, especially for a conscientious study of the principles and problems involved. They point out that the solution will have to be a *via media* between the extremes of unrestricted individualism, which rejects any governmental intervention and even any cooperation with organized labor, and extreme collectivism, which denies that there are any legitimate private interests, and subjects everything to a kind of economic dictatorship. There must be some planning, some ordering of competition in recognition of the fact that economic society forms a moral organism in which the relation of the individual members to one another is guided by their relation to the whole and its welfare. The quasi organic nature of civil and eco-

125

nomic society should find expression in a corresponding institutional set-up, one which does justice to the functional character and tasks of its members. What the bishops had in mind was, of course, the corporate order proposed in *Quadragesimo anno*, but they made it clear that any such functional reorganization would be ineffective if it is not preceded and accompanied by a spiritual reform. Functional representation, while more suitable than other types of social reorganization to counteract the evils of "bourgeois" liberalism and proletarian socialism, as a human institution is nevertheless by no means immune to abuse. The state as guardian and trustee of public welfare, thus, would still have to see to it that the organized "industries and professions" do not foster collective selfishness but adjust their particular interests to those of the national community.[277]

Pius XII on Industrial Relations

Pius XII, in an address to the *Union internationale des associations patronales catholiques*, on April 27, 1941, in a similar vein, stressed the intrinsic "community of interests and responsibilities in the work of the national economy." "Erroneous and baneful in its consequences," he said, "is the prejudice unfortunately too widespread, which sees in them [in the divergence of group goals] an irreducible opposition of conflicting interests." Actually they belong together and must be made to see their mutual interests. "Management and labor," for instance, "are not irreconcilable adversaries. They are cooperators in a mutual work." And if indeed they are cooperators, "why should it not be right to assign the workers a fair share of responsibility in the formation and the development of the national economy?"[278] Unfortunately, Pius XII said, the idea of "professional organization," which his predecessor put forth, awakened little echo. Instead, the unimaginative idea of state ownership and of nationalization came to the fore, probably because it seemed to offer immediate practical results.[279] Government ownership or, more often, control of public utilities is perfectly legitimate—but we ought not to forget that "the task of public rights is to serve, not to absorb, private rights."[280]

Pope Pius XII was always very specific and explicit in stressing the rights of private enterprise. Just as his predecessor, Pius XI, had emphasized that the wage contract is not *ipso facto* a contract of partnership, which gives the employee a claim of right to a share in the profits of his employer (64), so Pius XII rejects the idea "that any individual enterprise is by its nature a partnership where the relations between the partners are determined by the canons of distributive justice and where all, indiscriminately —whether owners or not of the means of production—have a right to their share of their property, or at least of the profits." But what is equally important is the fact, often overlooked by eager reformers, that for the same reasons employees have no implicit right to codetermine managerial policies: "Whoever owns the means of production . . . must be the master of his own economic decisions, though always within the limits of the public economic law." Yet, while the entrepreneur or corporate owners of a business are thus entitled to a fair return, the purpose of the social economy obliges them to set some of the earnings aside for the formation of capital or, to use the pope's own words, for "the increase of the national capital." It is at this point that Pius XII declares it as "most desirable that the workers also should contribute with the fruits of their savings to the formation of the national capital."[281] This proposition is in accordance with recent efforts in Europe toward an investment wage, which may be looked upon as a variation and possibly an extension of the security wage, demanded by the American bishops. It has been argued that the continued demands by labor for higher wages can be satisfied only if at least part of such increases be diverted to the formation of new capital in the interest of the continued economic welfare of the nation.

Pius XII's Message of Pentecost 1941

In a radio broadcast of June 1, 1941, commemorating the fiftieth anniversary of Rerum novarum, the Holy Father pointed out "that the economic wealth of a people does not properly consist in the abundance of goods, measured according to a purely material calculation of their value, but rather in that which such abundance represents and effectively provides, namely, an adequate material foundation for the proper personal development of its members. If such a fair distribution of goods is not realized or is only imperfectly achieved, the genuine aim of national economy has not been reached; since, however great the abundance of available goods, the people not participating in them would not be economically rich, but poor."[282] These observations, important as they are in regard to the problem of an investment wage, the consequent acquisition of productive property by the workers, and a corresponding share of labor in the management of such property, have meanwhile gained even greater importance in their bearing on the problem of the economic development of underprivileged countries.[283] The condition of these countries is often not so much a consequence of their lack of resources, or of their own political development, as it is the result of wanton exploitation by other nations, who developed resources for their own interest. Needless to say, the Church by defending the principle of private property does not wish to exonerate those who acquire property by fraud or violence or those who are quite willing to enjoy the privileges of ownership but refuse to acknowledge the social obligations that go with it. In other words, the Church "does not intend purely and simply to sustain the present state of affairs, as if she saw therein the expression of divine will, nor to protect, as a matter of principle, the rich and the plutocrat against the poor and the destitute." Neither does she entertain the notion that technological progress of necessity leads to business concentration, pushing "in its irresistible current all activity toward giant concerns and organizations, before which a social system founded on private property of the single individual must perforce collapse."[284] Technology is not fate, the pope says, but capable of and subject to regulation by the general good. If the service-function, the human and democratic nature of the economy is threatened, it is not on account of some anonymous and uncontrollable force, but on account of human self-seeking and lust for power. It is "threatened no less by monopoly, that is by the economic despotism of an anonymous conglomeration of private capital, than by the preponderance of organized masses, ready to use their power to the detriment of justice and the rights of others."[285] The economy is, of course, no less threatened by the political forces of collectivism which are "subjecting everything to state ownership and control, [reducing] the dignity of the human person almost to zero."[286] Unfortunately, even in the nations opposing communism, there is a tendency in the direction of state socialism. "In not a few countries," the pope stated at another occasion, "the modern State

128

is becoming a giant administrative machine. Its hand reaches into practically all facets of life: it attempts to make the entire scale of political, economic, social, and intellectual sectors its field of administration, even birth and death." Though seemingly caring for the welfare of its citizens from the cradle to the grave, to use an expression that was once applied to Lord Beveridge's plan for all-inclusive social security, the provider state creates an "impersonal climate which tends to penetrate and envelop all life," and in which "the sense of the common good becomes dull in the conscience of individuals . . ." The Holy Father speaks of a process of "depersonalization" which tends to deprive modern man of his distinctive personality. "In many of the most important activities of life," he says, "man has been reduced to a mere object of society, since society, in turn, is transformed into an impersonal system, a cold organization of forces."[287] The plight of the poor and of the lower middle classes, we are often told by the architects of a supposedly more progressive future, "cannot be treated as personal or individual." The solution is expected from an order, supposedly in the making, "a system which will be all-embracing and which, without basic prejudice to liberty, will lead men and things to a more united and growing force of action, making use of an ever more profound exploitation of technical progress." It seems that Pius XII had in mind those who steadfastly believe that our perfected knowledge of the behavior of the business cycle and our experience with the liberal use of monetary and fiscal policies will eventually provide us with the final answer to the social question: "When such a system shall be arrived at, salvation for all—it is said—shall gush forth automatically, ever improving living conditions and providing full employment everywhere."

Christian Aspects of the Problem of Full Employment

The Holy Father does not doubt the sincerity and the high ideals of those who hope and work for such a system, but he does doubt that a perpetual and unceasing improvement of the material standards of living and a correspondingly increasing demand for consumer goods will solve the problem of unemployment once and for all. He fears that this system will create a kind of spiral or some "sort of vicious circle, in which the end established and the means adopted pursue one another without ever coming together or reaching an accord."[288] While repeatedly stating that in the final analysis "full employment" is not merely a matter of economic techniques and skillful economic policy, but also and primarily one that concerns the social order as a whole, the pope is by no means unaware of the vital role of investment or capital formation for economic growth and social progress. "The solidarity of men among themselves demands," he said, "not only in the name of fraternal sentiment but also for reciprocal convenience itself, that all possibilities be employed to preserve existing jobs and create new ones. Therefore, those who can invest capital should consider, in view of the common good, whether, within the proportion and limits of their economic possibilities, and at opportune moments, they can reconcile with their conscience not making such investments and, through vain caution, withdraw into inactivity."[289]

However, when private initiative and free enterprise prove incapable of tackling the problem of unemployment, the government is obliged to step in and help through policy recommendation, direct assistance, public work projects, and the like.[290] The very dignity of labor makes it mandatory that all members of civil society make every effort to reduce unemployment to the very minimum. But the pope felt it necessary to call to the attention, especially of the "disillusioned" among Catholics, particularly among the youth, "that neither new laws nor new institutions are adequate to give to each the security to exist, protected against every misused restriction, and to develop with freedom in society." In this connection, Pius XII mentioned the arbitrary use of power by pressure groups, the corruption of public officials, the harmful role of party "politics" in public affairs, and the need for the formation of a public opinion which "points out, with frankness and courage, persons and situations which do not conform to just laws and institutions or which maliciously conceal the truth."[291] One of the ways and means of fostering civic-mindedness and social alertness and of creating an appropriate "climate" in the spheres of industry and social action is the formation of Catholic "cells" which could make their influence felt in the workshops, in neighborhoods, homes, and so on. Pius XII calls for lay apostles who would win back those of the laboring class who have lost their faith in the midst of what he calls the dangerous climate of industrial work. "There is, then, a need for thorough training in social doctrine," the pope said, "and for a Catholic workers' elite which will patiently draw labor organizations away from the influence of Marxism. Associations of Catholic workers are already producing remarkable results in many places."[292]

Interracial Justice

While Pope Pius XII in his address to the Second World Congress of the Lay Apostolate (October 5, 1957)—from which this last quotation was taken—pleaded particularly for the laboring masses of Latin America, the bishops of the United States pleaded the cause of the American Negroes, no less exposed to communist agitation. Already during the Second World War, in 1943, the American hierarchy had taken a stand in defense of interracial justice. Now once more, on November 13, 1958, they took up the problem of compulsory segregation. Having hoped in vain for quiet action, they now saw the need for serious exhortation. While they were far from suggesting further postponement of integration, they felt it their duty to warn against action without due deliberation and against outright recklessness in utter disregard for likely consequences. "We may well deplore a gradualism which is merely the cloak for inaction," they said. "But we equally deplore rash impetuosity that would sacrifice the achievement of decades in ill-timed and ill-considered ventures."[293]

To racial inequality and injustice there corresponds the apparent neglect of the family in public welfare and governmental social policies, which seem to address themselves preferably to the needy individual. Thus, in their pastoral letter on the Christian Family of November 21, 1949, the bishops declared that "when the aid of government is extended to those who raise crops or build machines but not to those who rear children, there exists a condition of inequality and even injustice." The bishops did not, of course, argue for direct governmental support of the family, regardless of need. They felt, however, that as it is the proper function of the state to protect the Church, in support of the basic freedom of worship, and the schools, so as to safeguard equal educational opportunity for all, so the government should also watch over the homes, the germ-cells of civil society and assist

131

all three "to discharge harmoniously their responsibilities in the best interest of public welfare."[294]

The American Bishops and Human Dignity

Closely linked with the existence and development of the family is the institution of private property.[295] In their joint pastoral letter of November 21, 1953, on the Dignity of Man, the bishops of the United States reaffirmed the right to property as a personal one, emphasizing, however, at the same time that "the use of property is also social." There can indeed be little doubt that the family derives much of its support and social vitality from ownership, just as it can hardly be denied that lack of property seriously endangers its social and spiritual welfare. Social security in the widest sense of the word is no satisfactory substitute for the family's quasi self-sufficiency and its own "home-made" security. Many are those, however, who nowadays are perfectly willing to turn the care of their aged parents, the welfare of surviving dependents, and the like entirely over to public institutions. This is but one aspect of the widespread belief that material security is all that is needed—a belief not far removed from the Marxian creed of temporal welfare. "But the exclusive dependence on economic security and social reform, to right the wrongs of mankind is by no means," the bishops state, "confined to Marxism. It affects the thought of great masses of men who reject the fundamental tenets of Marxism."[296]

Unfortunately, the general trend in the direction of "an excessive preoccupation with material security at the expense of spiritual well-being,"[297] has not been stemmed. There is little awareness among the people of the West that the so-called free world, in developing a predominantly "sensate culture," and in thoughtlessly accepting and clinging to the tenets of materialism, is actually admitting through the backdoor, as it were, the basic philosophy of communism which it fancies to fight at its front door. The materialistic philosophy of collectivism, however, finds its expression not merely in a preoccupation with nonmental values or with the material elements of culture, but also, if not primarily in the denial of the existence and efficacy of spiritual and supernatural forces and entities. To this corresponds, logically, a denial of the rational soul of man and his ability to engage, by himself, in free, responsible action. However, not only outright materialists, but an ever increasing number of people who, theoretically, do not deny the spiritual soul and the free will of man, are for all practical purposes shifting off their responsibility to collectivities such as the business corporation, the labor union, the political party, the social class to which they belong, or to the state. The collectivities and organizations, in turn, expect and tend to demand abject loyalty, eventually recognizing only one "virtue," namely the self-effacement of the individual, the surrender of his moral autonomy.

It is significant that the bishops of the United States in their statement On Individual Responsibility of November 19, 1960, express the opinion that "the foremost signs of the decline of personal responsibility are to be found in the family," especially in "the failure of parents to fulfill their responsibilities." "The individual person must assume as his proud right the accomplishment of whatever he can do for himself and for others, especially those of his family, and herein lies the importance of the Christian home."[298] "Equally conspicuous," the bishops go on to say, "is the evidence of decline in the sense of responsibility within our industrial organization and in our general economic life."[299] They deplore the growing pressures "for a constantly greater reliance on the collectivity rather than on the individual. An inordinate demand for benefits, most easily secured by the pressure of organization, has led an ever-growing number of our people to relinquish their rights and to abdicate their responsibilities. This concession creates a widening spiral of increasing demands and pressures with a further infringement on personal freedom and responsibility."

In view of the recent controversy on the concept and the function of "socialization," it is interesting that the American bishops years ago stated in so many words that while "intensive socialization can achieve mass benefits . . . man and morality can be seriously hurt in the process," if the latter is not "made to yield before the just and determined wills of individual persons."[300] They quoted Pius XII, who in a letter of July 12, 1960, to the Social Week in Grenoble, France, had pointed out that it is possible for man to control the process of socialization, preventing it from "increasing constantly in its breadth and depth" and from one day reducing men to the role of automatons. "For socialization is not

133

the result of forces of nature acting according to a determination that cannot be changed. It is the work of man, of a free being conscious of and responsible for its acts."[301]

The Rise of an American Catholic Social Movement

If one compares the attitude of the Church in America toward the social question in the years after World War I, especially since the Great Depression, with that of the time before the Great War, one cannot possibly fail to notice a decided change. In the nineteenth century, which—seen from the viewpoint of the history of ideas—lasted till World War I, and before, individual bishops occasionally took a stand, as a rule with regard to some specific social problem, such as problems of labor and industrial relations. As a matter of fact, social Catholicism in pre-First-World-War America was largely a matter of personalities. There was no Catholic social movement if by social movement we mean group action for social reform. Even the Central Verein, being a "roof-organization" or federation of Catholic insurance fraternities rather than an association of its own, can hardly be looked upon as representing a "movement" of this kind. Perhaps one can say that it provided for the first time in the history of American Catholicism organized leadership in matters of social action. It is doubtful whether without the genius of Frederick P. Kenkel, without the Central Bureau, a clearing house of social action, without the *Central-Blatt and Social Justice* the Central Union would ever have been in the forefront of American social Catholicism. In other words, even in this case it was a matter of one man, a pioneer, and a small coterie of disciples and collaborators. Pursuing a somewhat conservative course, this group was not as vocal and demonstrative as it might otherwise have been. There was something "academic" in the best sense of the word in their endeavors, a stress on principles rather than on policies, on the over-all picture rather than on technical details. Being conservative never meant an unproductive negativism or lack of vigor or dynamics. It meant a cautious attitude toward any kind of boisterous activism or of mere pragmatism which produced energy without direction. But it never lacked in determination to help restore modern society to Christ. The word "social justice" in the title of its magazine was never an empty phrase, yet it meant de-

cidedly, and from the beginning, the realization of justice in society through the concerted effort of all of its members, from the
grass roots upward to the state as the divinely instituted guardian
of public welfare—never merely from the top downward by legislative policies and administrative action.

On the liberal side of social Catholicism in this country there
was from the beginning a sense of what may be called compas-
sionate impatience, saying with the Lord: "I am moved with pity
for the multitude . . . they have nothing to eat . . . (while you
are defining social justice, quibble about the meaning of "socialization," or try to determine the limits of government intervention) . . . they may faint on their way home." (Mark 8:2). Perhaps there is a real need for such ferment and eagerness in any
social movement. And a movement it now is. Largely under the
auspices of the Social Action Department of the National Catholic Welfare Conference there has in the last few decades been a
veritable spring of Catholic societies devoted to one or the other
aspect of the social question. In some cases both John A. Ryan
and Frederick P. Kenkel stood as godfathers to a new organization. The history of such dynamic and inspiring organizations as
the National Catholic Rural Life Conference, the National Catholic Conference for Interracial Justice, the Young Christian Workers, the Association of Catholic Trade Unionists, the Catholic
Council on Working Life, the Catholic Labor Guild, the Catholic Employers, Managers and Technologists Study Groups, the
Christian Family Life Movement, the Grail, the Catholic Worker
and numerous Catholic professional organizations is still to be
written. Such histories are likely to be largely biographies of such
great leaders as Bishop Francis J. Haas; Archbishop Edwin
V. O'Hara, until his death honorary president of the American
Catholic Sociological Society; Aloisius Cardinal Muench, for many
years honorary chairman of the Social Action Committee of the
Central Verein; Bishop Bernard J. Sheil; Virgil Michel, O.S.B.,
who with Father (later Msgr.) Martin B. Hellriegel, demonstrated
the theological roots of social thought; John La Farge, S.J.; Msgr.
Luigi G. Ligutti; Msgr. Daniel M. Cantwell; Edgar Schmiedeler,
O.S.B.; Edward A. Marciniak; Dorothy Day; Peter Maurin; Dr.
Lydwine van Kersbergen—to mention only a few. There is no esti-
mate as to what the founders and such leading members of the
American Catholic Sociological Society, as Ralph A. Gallagher,

S.J.; Dr. Eva J. Ross; Msgr. Paul H. Furfey; Raymond W. Murray, C.S.C.; John L. Thomas, S.J.; Dr. Clement S. Mihanovich; Dr. Alphonse H. Clemens; Brother Gerald J. Schnepp, S.M.; Joseph H. Fichter, S.J., and many others have done for the status of Catholic sociologists in the academic community and for the scientific foundations of Catholic social action. The same is, of course, true of the Catholic Economic Association whose first honorary president was Msgr. John A. Ryan. Here men like Thomas F. Divine, S.J.; Bernard J. Dempsey, S.J.; Dr. Edward H. Chamberlain; Dr. Raymond J. Saulnier; Sr. M. Yolande Schulte, O.S.F.; Dr. Goetz Briefs; John F. Cronin, S.S.; Dr. Joseph Solterer; Dr. Walter Froehlich; Leo C. Brown, S.J., have made a truly inestimable contribution to both the recognition of the Catholic economist among his non-Catholic colleagues and to the recognition of the relative autonomy of economics as a science among Catholics at large. It will be for later generations of Catholic social actionists and Catholic social scientists to uncover and demonstrate the historical role which—directly or indirectly—the two great men of social Catholicism in America, Frederick P. Kenkel and John A. Ryan, have played in the rise and growth of the Catholic social movement of this country, represented in the numerous organizations, many of which could, for lack of space, not even be mentioned.

New Horizons

Ryan and Kenkel, one representing the liberal, the other the conservative, school of Catholic social reform, have since gone to their eternal reward. They may now smile—if such would be possible—about the mutual suspicions of Catholic "liberals" and "conservatives." But those of us who are pledged to carry on the work of Catholic social action should be aware of the fact that the future is pregnant with problems that probably cannot be solved with tools of the past. Automation for one thing is almost certain to change the role of the unions. Technological unemployment will, in the long run, not respond to deficit spending and monetary policies. Even the traditional concepts of property seem no longer to serve the understanding of the far-reaching changes that are rapidly taking place under our very eyes.[302] The question is being asked repeatedly and ever more anxiously: What is the essential difference, if any, between the manager of a "capitalistic" corporation, possibly owned by a pension or welfare fund, and the manager of a government-controlled enterprise in Russia? Is there a chance that the two worlds, the "West" and the "East" are closer together than they suspect? The Church has indeed never taught that our prevailing economic system is a divine dispensation or that capitalism is a dictate of the natural law.[303] Institutions change, and so do economic and political systems. Rarely do they change without violent birth pangs. What counts is the spirit. Where the Church is, there is Christ.

NOTES

1. "Since this nature is social, it will manifest its weakness and fundamental disorder in its social relations . . ." (Daniel A. O'Connor, C.S.V., *Catholic Social Doctrine* [Westminster, Md.: Newman, 1956], p. 7). See also Johannes Messner, *Social Ethics* (St. Louis: Herder, 1949), pp. 253 ff.
2. *De veritate*, 11, 1.
3. *Summa contra gentiles*, III, 69. According to St. Thomas, "to detract from the creature's perfection is to detract from the perfection of divine power" and "it is derogatory to the divine goodness to deny things their proper operations."
4. St. Augustine, *The City of God*, XII, 11, 13; Modern Library ed. (New York: Random House, 1950), pp. 391, 393. St. Augustine did not achieve the degree of historical understanding demonstrated by Otto of Freising; cf. *The Two Cities*, ed. A. P. Evans and C. Knapp (New York: Columbia, 1928); also Augustine, *Der Sabbat Gottes*, ed. Herman Hefele (Stuttgart: Frommanns, 1923), p. 15.
5. Wilhelm Windelband says of Greek philosophy that it had "from the beginning directed its questions with reference to the φύσις, abiding essence, and this mode of stating the question, which proceeded from the need of apprehending Nature, had influenced the progress of forming conceptions so strongly that the chronological course of events had always been treated as something having no metaphysical interest of its own. In this connection Greek science regarded not only the individual man, but also the human race, with all its fortunes, deeds, and experiences, as ultimately but an episode, a special formation of the world process which repeats itself forever according to like laws." Plato does ask the question as to what is the final purpose of man's earthly life, and Aristotle seeks the laws which seem to determine the sequence of political formations, but "the inquiry for a meaning in *human history taken as a whole*, for a connected plan of historical development, had never once been put forward, and still less had it occurred to any of the old thinkers to see in *this* [italics added] the intrinsic, essential nature of the world" (*A History of Philosophy* [New York: Macmillan, 1914], p. 255). Cf. also P. Teilhard de

137

Chardin, S.J., *The Phenomenon of Man* (New York: Harper, 1961), pp. 303 ff; Robert T. Francoeur, "For Teilhard, No Flight from Time," *Catholic World*, 193, pp. 367 ff.; Luigi Sturzo, *Inner Laws of Society* (New York: Kenedy, 1944), pp. xxx–xxxvi; Karl Löwith, *Meaning in History* (Chicago: Chicago, 1950), pp. 160–173; Wilhelm Kahles, *Die Geschichtstheologie des Rupertus von Deutz* (Münster: Aschendorf, 1960).

6. Robert Grosche, *Pilgernde Kirche* (Freiburg: Herder, 1938), pp. 1–22. The notion, which Western civilization has inherited from Greek philosophy, viz., that reasoning from particulars to generals is necessarily a progression toward a greater degree of reality and truth, seems long overdue for another Catholic re-examination.

7. *Loc. cit.*, pp. 256, 257, 260, 262. This writer has taken the liberty of revising the translation of some of the passages quoted, comparing them with the German original and rendering them somewhat more freely.

8. *Mater et Magistra*, 236 and 238.

9. *Summa theol.*, I–II, 14, 1 and 3.

10. Bernard Wuellner, S.J., *Dictionary of Scholastic Philosophy* (Milwaukee: Bruce, 1956), p. 29.

11. Yves Simon, *Nature and Function of Authority* (Milwaukee: Marquette, 1940), p. 27.

12. Pius XII used this useful illustration *before* he was raised to the papacy. A more accurate account of it can be found in the book on the ethics of the stock and commodity exchanges, the *Börsenmoral* by Oswald von Nell-Breuning, S.J. (Freiburg: Herder, 1928) pp. 15 f.

13. *In Epist. Joannis ad Parthos*, tr. VII, 8.

14. "It is faith . . . that brings life to the just man" (Gal. 3:11; cf. Heb. 10:38).

15. Josef Pieper, *Prudence* (New York: Pantheon, 1959), p. 90.

16. *Summa theol.* I–II, 108, 1.

17. Cf. Karl Adam, *The Spirit of Catholicism* (London: Sheed & Ward, 1929), pp. 176 ff, and 193 ff. In his address of October 11, 1962, inaugurating the Second Vatican Council, Pope John XXIII stated that while the Church desires to show herself as the loving mother of all, she "does not offer modern man riches nor promise them mere earthly happiness. Rather she distributes to them the goodness of divine grace . . . [which] raises them to the dignity of the sons of God." But "through her children, she spreads everywhere the fullness of Christian charity. Nothing is more effective than this in eradicating the seeds of discord; nothing is more efficacious in promoting concord, just peace, and the fraternal union of all men."

18. Heinrich Keller, S.J., and Oswald von Nell-Breuning, S.J., *Das Recht der Laien in der Kirche* (Heidelberg: Kerle, 1950), p. 90.

19. Oswald von Nell-Breuning, S.J., *Wirtschaft und Gesellschaft Heute*, II (Freiburg: Herder, 1957), 382.

20. "The Church—Foundation of Society, Allocution of Pope Pius XII to the College of Cardinals at a Public Consistory, Febr. 20, 1946," *The Catholic Mind*, 44 (1946), p. 201.

21. At the fifty-second annual convention of the Catholic Press Association in Boston, May 17, 1962, Cardinal Cushing referred to the scriptural metaphor of the shepherd and his flock. With the passing

of time, he said, the emphasis has shifted from the pastoral care of Our Lord for his own to the metaphor's sheep and those qualities which are usually associated with the meekness of the lamb: lack of courage, general docility, and lack of spirit. "It has been assumed that these qualities were the proper qualities of the humble layman . . . Time and events have now made it necessary for us to take a new measure of the place of the Catholic lay person in the Mystical Body of Christ and to discover what contribution the educated and dedicated layman can provide in working out God's plan for his kingdom among men . . . In order to convince the timid, it is going to be necessary to demonstrate that the Church itself vitally needs this help in order to function effectively and that with it new vistas open for its expansion and progress." *The Catholic Bulletin* (St. Paul) (May 25, 1962), pp. 1, 12.

22. *Wirtschaft und Gesellschaft Heute, loc. cit.,* p. 363.

23. Franz H. Mueller, "What the Encyclicals Do Not Teach," *Social Justice Review,* 34 (1941), 43 ff. Cf. René Brouillard, S.J., who in 1927 wrote: "The Church in presenting her rules of individual ethics does not want to suppress medicine and hygiene, and neither those of psychology and the art of pedagogy. Likewise, in establishing her social theology, she does not mean to supersede the art of government and the practice of politics. Much more, she recognizes that each of the purely secular provinces of learning and action has a sphere proper to itself which does not concern her other than indirectly, namely by reason of its moral and religious implications" (*Études,* 191 [1927], 397).

24. Pieper, *Prudence,* p. 97. In the last sentence quoted, the translation followed the German text too closely. It seems grammatically more satisfactory to say, "can ever—in *any* 'concrete situation' . . ."

25. *Ibid.,* pp. 50 f. and 88 f.

26. O'Connor, *Catholic Social Doctrine,* p. 70. Father O'Connor continues as follows: "Inasmuch as they write for the whole world, the popes must carefully restrict themselves to more or less general directives that everyone must accept and adapt to the particular circumstances of time and place. *They do not dispense us from thinking for ourselves;* what they require of us is not blind devotion to each word, but fidelity to the inspiration contained in the message" (italics added).

27. Actually, economics and sociology now put their pride in throwing out all historical and institutional considerations and reducing their disciplines to quasi natural sciences, whose "laws" are valid under all circumstances of time and space.

28. This statement is certain to meet with sharp opposition simply because we have come to apply the term "state" to any kind of political organization be it a polis, empire, kingdom, republic, nation, realm, commonwealth, or principality. Of course, man as a political being has always lived under some form of government, but the modern "state" is a product of the civilization of the Renaissance.

29. Cf. Franz H. Mueller, "The Development of the Modern Dualism between State and Society," *American Catholic Sociological Review,* 4, pp. 185–193. Lorenz von Stein (1815–1890) was probably the first to realize and theorize upon this dualism; cf. W. A. Dunning,

A *History of Political Theories from Rousseau to Spencer* (New York: Macmillan, 1933), pp. 377–386.

30. Talcott Parsons, "Society," *Encyclopaedia of the Social Sciences* (1st ed.), 14, 266; cf. also Franz H. Mueller, "The Rise of Modern Society," *American Catholic Sociological Review*, 6, pp. 33–41.

31. So L. A. Loser in his introduction to Max Scheler's *Ressentiment* (New York: Free Press, 1961), p. 13.

32. From Max Weber, *Essays in Sociology*, translated, edited, and with an introduction by H. H. Gerth and C. Wright Mills (New York: Oxford, 1946), p. 183. Following in the footsteps of Tönnies, Max Weber calls a social relationship "communal," "if and so far as the orientation of social action—whether in the individual case, on the average, or in the pure type—is based on the subjective feelings of the parties, whether affectional or traditional, that they belong together. A social relationship will, on the other hand, be called 'associative' [the 'societal action' of above], if and in so far as the orientation of social action within it rests on a rationally motivated agreement, whether the basis of rational judgment be absolute values or reasons of expediency" (M. Weber, *The Theory of Social and Economic Organization* [New York: Oxford, 1947], p. 136).

33. For a more complete study of the historical origins of modern society, consult Alfred von Martin, *Sociology of the Renaissance* (New York: Oxford, 1944), and B. Groethuysen, *Origines de l'esprit bourgeois en France*, I (Paris: Gallimard, 1927); cf. also Mueller, "The Rise of Modern Society," *loc. cit.*

34. Ferdinand Tönnies in his *Fundamental Concepts of Sociology* (New York: American Book, 1940), p. 39, quotes this passage from an article by Bluntschli in the *Deutsche Staatswörterbuch*, which B. co-edited. In his *Theory of the State* (Oxford: Clarendon, 1885), p. 104, Bluntschli refers to society as "a shifting conglomeration of individuals." —Probably the first to draw a distinction between the two opposing concepts of civil and political society was A. L. von Schlözer (1735–1809). Long before Tawney, R. von Gneist (1816–95) called modern society an acquisitive one. The real pioneer work in the sociological analysis of modern society, however, was done by Georg W. F. Hegel (1770–1831), Robert von Mohl (1799–1875), and Lorenz von Stein (1815–1890). There have been related studies by J. M. Baldwin, C. H. Cooley, R. M. MacIver, W. G. Sumner, and Lester F. Ward. The classic by Tönnies *Gemeinschaft und Gesellschaft* (the translation of which has been mentioned in the beginning of this footnote) presents a predominantly systematic, not a historical treatment of the matter. Josef Pieper in his *Grundformen sozialer Spielregeln*, (Freiburg: Herder, 1933), has shown the societal pattern of interhuman behavior to be a legitimate and necessary one, provided it does not overwhelm certain other patterns of equal legitimacy (*op. cit.*, pp. 56–60); cf. also Franz H. Mueller, "On Some Basic Patterns of Interhuman Behavior," *American Catholic Sociological Review*, 6, pp. 232–241.

35. Cf. Robert M. MacIver, "Sociology," *Encyclopaedia of the Social Sciences* (1st ed.), 14, 244; Tönnies, *Fundamental Concepts*, p. 29.

36. Henry Sumner Maine, *Ancient Law* (New York: Holt, 1875), p. 165; Paul P. Harbrecht, S.J., and Adolf A. Berle, *Toward a Para-*

proprietal Society (New York: Twentieth Century Fund, 1960), pp. 37 ff.

37. Talcott Parsons, *Essays in Sociological Theory* (rev. ed.; Glencoe, Ill.: Free Press, 1958), pp. 130, 117.

38. According to Talcott Parsons, anomy may perhaps most briefly be characterized as "the state where large numbers of individuals are to a serious degree lacking in the kind of integration with stable institutional patterns which is essential to their own personal stability and to the smooth functioning of the social system" (*Essays*, p. 125).

39. Frank Tannenbaum, "The Social Function of Trade Unionism," *Political Science Quarterly*, 62 (1947), 163.

40. *Ibid.*, pp. 168, 190; "the very forces of industrialism," says Tannenbaum on p. 182, "that destroyed the older order have laid the basis for the new one." Similarly, Peter Drucker, *The New Society* (New York: Harper, 1950), pp. 151 ff.

41. "Social Function," p. 164.

42. *Ibid.*, p. 166.

43. *Ibid.*, p. 166.

44. *Ibid.*, p. 167.

45. *Ibid.*, p. 188.

46. Cf. Franz H. Mueller, "Ordered Consumption via Ordered Production," *The Guildsman* (Germantown, Ill.), 6, 8 (May, 1938), 2–5.

47. "Social Function," pp. 174 f.

48. *Ibid.*, p. 175.

49. *Ibid.*, p. 182.

50. Drucker, *New Society*, p. 154.

51. *Ibid.*, p. 151.

52. *Ibid.*, p. 153.

53. *Ibid.*, p. 152.

54. Hans Bokelmann, "Christliches Selbstverständnis vor Gott und Gegenwart," *Frankfurter Hefte*, 16, pp. 655–666.

55. Hans Wulf, S.J., "Die Enzyklika 'Mater et Magistra' im Kreuzfeuer der Kritik," *Stimmen der Zeit*, 169 (1962), 260.

56. F. L. Nussbaum, *A History of the Economic Institutions of Modern Europe*, (New York: Crofts, 1933).

57. These latter terms are here used in a looser sense than they are used in the well-known books by Burnham and Boulding. Cf. James Burnham, *The Managerial Revolution*, (New York: John Day, 1941); Kenneth E. Boulding, *The Organizational Revolution*, (New York: Harper, 1953).

58. Werner Sombart, *Weltanschauung, Science and Economy* (New York: Veritas, 1939), p. 5. Cf. also Sombart, "Capitalism," *Encyclopaedia of the Social Sciences* (1st ed.), 3, 196b.

59. E.g., *Summa theol.*, II–II, q. 32, a.5, a.6, a.9; q. 108, a.1; q. 118, a.1; q. 169, a. 1.

60. Medieval moralists considered accumulation of money permissible if and insofar such means were intended to serve gifted men of high virtue to reach a higher status. Such rise was considered unjustified if it was merely to satisfy a vaulting ambition rather than a sincere desire to serve one's fellow men by making a better use of one's capacities.

61. Sombart, "Capitalism," pp. 196–198.

62. It is difficult to see how so able an economist as the late Bernard W. Dempsey, S.J., could seriously insist that "there is no such thing as capitalism," as he did in his otherwise excellent book, *The Functional Economy*, (Englewood Cliffs, N.J.: Prentice-Hall, 1958), pp. 148–163.

63. Bede Jarrett, O.P., *S. Antonino and Medieval Economics* (St. Louis: Herder, 1914), pp. xiv f.; Also, G. M. Modlin and F. T. de Vyver, *Development of Economic Society* (Boston: Heath, 1946), p. 111.

64. Nussbaum, *History*, pp. 64 f.

65. E. F. Heckscher, quoting Mandeville, in Henry W. Spiegel (ed.), *The Development of Economic Thought* (New York: Wiley, 1952), p. 41.

66. ". . . *usus pecuniae est in emissione ipsius.*" *Summa theol.* II–II, q. 117, a.4 c; there St. Thomas also says that "to spend money usefully is more prudent than to keep it usefully."

67. Gustav Schmoller, *The Mercantile System* (New York: Peter Smith, 1931), p. 51.

68. Arthur Salz, *Macht und Wirtschaftsgesetz* (Leipzig: Teubner, 1930), pp. 145 f.

69. L. B. Packard, *The Commercial Revolution*, (New York: Holt, 1927), p. 21.

70. Cf. J. B. Kraus, S.J., *Scholastik, Puritanismus und Kapitalismus* (Munich: Dunker & Humblot, 1930), pp. 88 ff.

71. Robert L. Heilbroner, *The Making of Economic Society* (Englewood Cliffs, N.J.: Prentice-Hall, 1962), pp. 53 f.; cf. also R. H. Tawney, *Religion and the Rise of Capitalism* (New York: New American Library, 1961), p. 58.

72. Hedwig Brey, *Hochscholastik und 'Geist' des Kapitalismus* (Leipzig: Noske, 1927), p. 73.

73. Carl Ilgner, *Die volkswirtschaftlichen Anschauungen Antonins von Florenz* (Paderborn: Schöningh, 1904), pp. 18, 42; Jarrett, *S. Antonino*, p. 67; Edmund Schreiber, *Die volkswirtschaftlichen Anschauungen der Scholastic seit Thomas v. Aquin* (Jena: Fischer, 1913), p. 222; Max Scheler, *Vom Umsturz der Werte*, II (Leipzig: Neue Geist, 1919), pp. 310 f.; also cf., *Summa theol.*, II–II, q. 78, a,2.

74. Bede Jarrett, O.P., quotes a passage which could be interpreted to mean that Antonine rejected any income not earned by labor or service: "If . . . the trader seeks a moderate profit for the purpose of providing for himself and family according to the condition becoming to their state of life, or to enable him to aid the poor more generously, or even if he goes into commerce for the common good (lest, for example, the State should be without what its life requires), and consequently seeks a profit not as an ultimate end but merely as a *wage of labor* [emphasis added], he cannot in that case be condemned" (*Summa Moralis*, II, i, 16, ii). B. Jarrett, *Social Theories of the Middle Ages* (Westminster, Md.: Newman, 1942), p. 156. Had St. Antonine been an economist, aware of what he was saying, he could be assumed to have implied that labor is the only source of value, but in the context of his teaching it seems unlikely that he actually entertained such thought. At any rate this passage does demonstrate that his concept of

profit was hardly "revolutionary" or departing from the classic scholastic tradition.

75. Cf. Amintore Fanfani, *Catholicism, Protestantism, and Capitalism*, (New York: Sheed & Ward, 1939), p. 130.

76. E. Salin, "Just Price," *Encyclopaedia of the Social Sciences* (1st ed.), 8, 506b; Selma Hagenauer, *Das "justum pretium" bei Thomas von Aquino* (Stuttgart: Kohlhammer, 1931), pp. 104 ff.

77. This is Joseph Schumpeter's concept of our prevailing economic system; cf. *Economic Journal*, 38, no. 151.

78. Cf. August M. Knoll, *Der Zins in der Scholastik* (Innsbruck: Tyrolia, 1933), pp. 67 f. Among the legal devices used to avoid a conflict with the canonical prohibition of interest were the rent purchase or perpetuity (*census hereditarius*) and the personal rent or terminable annuity (*census personalis utrimque redimibilis*). Both granted a rent charge on real estate for the loan of a capital sum. The bull, *Cum onus*, of Pius V (1569) and *Detestabilis avaritiae* of Sixtus V (1586) did not generally condemn these mortgagelike devices. *Vix pervenit* seems to formally permit them, for the encyclical speaks of contracts which are totally different from the contract of *mutuum* and which permit lawful investment of funds, e.g., in order to secure an annuity or to engage in licit business transactions from which to derive a fair profit. There are several decrees by Pius VIII (1829–1830) and Gregory XVI (1831–1846) which admonish all concerned not to disquiet debtors, creditors, and their confessors, provided they have the intention to submit to the ordinances of the Holy See: "Non esse inquietandos, et acquiescant, dummodo parati sint stare mandatis sanctae Sedis." Cf. A. M. Knoll, *Der soziale Gedanke im modernen Katholizismus* (Vienna: Reinhold, 1932), pp. 28–31.

79. Goetz Briefs of Georgetown feels that there was a real shift of emphasis between the sixteenth and eighteenth centuries to what he calls "marginal ethics." He gives weighty reasons for his assumption, quoting Cardinal Cajetan and referring to Tomas de Mercado to show that in the era of "baroque ethics" (Werner Schoellgen) contemporary Christian writers did adopt a capitalistic ethos; cf. Goetz A. Briefs, "The Ethos Problem in the Present Pluralistic Society," *Review of Social Economy*, 15, 1 (March, 1957), esp. 50 f.

80. Interest must not be confused with *interesse*, a compensation for loss. The scholastics called interest for a loan of money *usura*. Usury, thus, is not excessive interest, but any payment exacted on the basis of an alleged productivity of money as money, or for a consumptive loan.

81. The main "titles" (to a compensation, not to interest in the sense of usury) are: risk of nonrepayment; missing an opportunity for other lawful gain; a positive loss due to the illiquidity caused by the loan; and belated repayment. Actually, the term *interesse* seems to have been derived from the words, *quod inter est*, that is, the time "which lies between" the due date and the date of actual repayment.

82. Werner Sombart, *The Quintessence of Capitalism* (New York: Dutton, 1915), p. 247. In the (original) German edition of this book, published under the title, *Der Bourgeois* (Munich: Duncker & Humblot, 1913), this reference can be found on p. 317. This is not to minimize the importance, even in precapitalistic times, of commercial

credit as demonstrated in the bottomries, *collegantia, commenda, societas maris*, etc., known long before the rise of capitalism. Perhaps the answer to this is in Arthur Salz's observation that trade is "the capitalistic profession of the Middle Ages." Cf. also Franz Schaub, *Der Kampf gegen den Zinswucher, ungerechten Preis und unlauteren Handel im Mittelalter* (Freiburg: Herder, 1905), pp. 157–161.

83. Sombart, *Quintessence*, p. 246.

84. Henry W. Spiegel in *The Development*, p. 23, states that a great part of medieval industry was a "system of organized monopolies, endowed with a public status." But the absence of competition does not turn an economic organization necessarily into a monopoly, at least not into one meant to control supply for the purpose of regulating prices.

85. Cf. the article on property by Léon de Sousberghe, S.J., *Nouvelle revue théologique*, (1950), 580–607.

86. Eric E. Lampard, *Industrial Revolution*, (Washington, D.C.: American Historical, 1957), p. 10, speaks of a "transformation of medieval lordship into something resembling landlordship."

87. Alfons Steinmann, *Sklavenlos und Alte Kirche* (München-Gladbach: Volksvereins, 1922), p. 119.

88. Jarrett, *Social Theories*, pp. 103, 121.

89. Hans Hausherr, *Wirtschaftsgeschichte der Neuzeit* (Köln: Böhlau, 1960), p. 55; Samuel E. Morison, *Christopher Columbus, Mariner* (New York: New American Library, 1961), p. 86, states that Isabella eventually forbade the slave trade, "but not until it had proved to be unprofitable."

90. "Some Social and Moral Implications of American Negro Slavery" (Unpublished dissertation, Catholic University, Washington, D.C., 1926), p. 15; Msgr. Gilligan's source for the last quotation is *Collectanea S. Congregationis de Propaganda Fide*, 1, 76. Eric Williams, *Capitalism and Slavery* (New York: Russell & Russell, 1961), p. 42, insists that "the Church also supported the slave trade" without giving any verifiable historical proof whatsoever.

91. "Mercantilism," *Encyclopaedia of the Social Sciences* (1st ed.), 10, 338b.

92. William D. Gramp, "The Liberal Elements in English Mercantilism," *The Quarterly Journal of Economics*, 56 (1952), 487.

93. Frank A. Neff, *Economic Doctrines* (New York: McGraw-Hill, 1950), p. 481.

94. *Theory of Moral Sentiments* (London, 1759), Part IV, ch. 1; *An Inquiry into the Nature and Causes of the Wealth of Nations* (London, 1776), Book IV, ch. 2.

95. Algie Martin Simons, *Social Forces in American History* (New York: Macmillan, 1911), pp. 70, 71, 254 f. Cf. also Harold J. Faulkner, *Economic History* (8th ed.; New York: Harper, 1960), pp. 127 f.

96. George Soule and Vincent Carosso, *American Economic History*, (New York: Holt, Rinehart & Winston, 1961), p. 54.

97. Georg Jellinek, *The Declaration of the Rights of Man and of Citizens* (New York: Holt, 1901). Important in this connection is the role of Lafayette, who had, on the side of George Washington, fought for American independence and who was largely responsible for the Declaration of Rights in 1789.

98. Shepard B. Clough and Charles W. Cole, *Economic History of Europe* (Boston: Heath, 1946), p. 422.

99. Frederick C. Dietz, *The Industrial Revolution* (New York: Holt, 1927), pp. 28 ff.

100. Eric E. Lampard, *Industrial Revolution*, (Washington, D.C.: American Historical, 1957), pp. 19–21.

101. Neff, *Economic Doctrines*, p. 97; John F. Bell, *A History of Economic Thought* (New York: Ronald, 1953), p. 156.

102. Eric Roll, *A History of Economic Thought* (Englewood Cliffs, N.J.: Prentice-Hall, 1956), p. 138.

103. Nussbaum, *History*, p. 153.

104. *Worldly Philosophers* (New York: Simon & Schuster, 1953), p. 31. Heilbroner can hardly have had a good reason for withholding his source, viz., Bernard Mandeville.

105. *Ibid.*, p. 32.

106. Arnold Toynbee, *Lectures on the Industrial Revolution of the Eighteenth Century in England* (London: Longmans, Green, 1913); cf. also Henry Mayhew, *London Labor and the London Poor* (London: Griffin, Bohn, 1861/62). Hood's "Song of the Shirt," Hans Christian Andersen's "Matchgirl," and Elizabeth Barrett Browning's "The Cry of the Children" illustrate some of the human suffering which followed the Industrial Revolution and the uninhibited application of the principle of *laissez faire*.

107. Frederick M. Eden, *The State of the Poor*, 3 vols. (London: B. & J. White, 1797), 2A2 (this citation is the one given by Anton von Kostanecki, *Arbeit und Armut* [Freiburg: Herder, 1909], p. 52.)

108. Cf. Andrew M. Greeley, "The Question of the Parish as a Community," *Worship*, 36, p. 137. If, as Father Greeley believes, the theory of mass society has come under attack, it is in all likelihood because of a gradual change in the fact situation. But *that* mass society was already a reality in the age of full capitalism.

109. Cf. G. Briefs, *The Proletariat* (New York: McGraw-Hill, 1937), pp. 67 ff; Franz Müller (Franz H. Mueller), "Zur Beurteilung des Kapitalismus in der Katholischen Publizistik des 19. Jahrhunderts," in W. Schwer and Franz Müller, *Der Deutsche Katholizismus im Zeitalter des Kapitalismus* (Augsburg: Haas & Grabherr, 1932), pp. 83 f., 86 f., 217.

110. Georgiana Putnam McEntee, *The Social Catholic Movement in Great Britain* (New York: Macmillan, 1927), p. 1.

111. John M. Clark, *Competition as a Dynamic Process*, (Washington, D.C.: Brookings, 1961), p. 24; Overton H. Taylor, *A History of Economic Thought* (New York: McGraw-Hill, 1960), pp. 86 f., says that "the 'conversion' of the nineteenth century British business community to economic liberalism was due less to the influence of the teachings of the country's liberal economists than to the currently existing situation for its industrial capitalists which made those teachings acceptable to them, i.e., in accord with their self-interests as long as that was their situation."

112. Joseph Schumpeter, *The Theory of Economic Development* (Cambridge, Mass.: Harvard, 1934), p. 66; Franz Müller (Franz H. Mueller), *Der kapitalistische Unternehmer* (Würzburg: Das Neue Volk, 1926).

145

113. Heilbroner, *The Making*, pp. 64 ff. The term, "command economy," is also used by William Ebenstein, *Today's Isms* (Englewood Cliffs, N.J.: Prentice-Hall, 1958), p. 157, and in George N. Halm's *Economic Systems* (New York, Holt, Rinehart & Winston, 1960), pp. 237–252.

114. Weber, *Essays*, p. 371.

115. *Ibid.*, p. 331.

116. Cf. the special issue of the *Review of Social Economy*, 15 (March, 1957), dealing with the problem of marginal ethos.

117. M. Christina Schwartz, *The Catholic Church Working Through its Individual Members in any Age and Nation makes a Positive Social Contribution as Seen in France 1815–1870*, (Washington, D.C.: Catholic University, 1939), p. 2.

118. Charity, since in its theological sense it is identical with the Christian life, presupposes, even includes, the justice which plays a decisive role in social action.

119. Celestine J. Nuesse, *The Social Thought of American Catholics 1634–1829* (Washington, D.C.: Catholic University, 1945), pp. 281, 7.

120. *Ibid.*, pp. 99, 131, 211.

121. *Ibid.*, p. 218.

122. *Ibid.*, p. 226.

123. *Ibid.*, pp. 285, 218, 282.

124. *Ibid.*, pp. 131, 269; cf. also John O'Grady, *Catholic Charities in the United States*, (Washington, D.C.: Catholic Charities, 1931).

125. Nuesse, *Social Thought*, p. 282.

126. *Ibid.*, p. 283.

127. *Ibid.*, pp. 255, 233, 238, 89. FitzSimons was not motivated by ethical concerns about *laissez faire*, but considered protection a policy more favorable to business interest. Cf. also Henry W. Spiegel, *The Rise of American Economic Thought* (Philadelphia: Chilton, 1960), pp. 47 ff.

128. Nuesse, *Social Thought*, pp. 260–272.

129. *Ibid.*, p. 261; Cf. also Theodore Maynard, *The Story of American Catholicism* (New York: Macmillan, 1942), p. 343.

130. Nuesse, *Social Thought*, pp. 342 f. and 297.

131. *Ibid.*, p. 246.

132. Maynard, *Story*, p. 344.

133. *Ibid.*, p. 345.

134. Nuesse, *Social Thought*, pp. 165 f.

135. *Ibid.*, p. 154.

136. Many pastors, however, opposed the colonization project which they thought would depopulate their parishes, and would make it impossible for them to pay the large debts which the parishes, had incurred for church buildings, schools, etc. Archbishop John Hughes of New York considered the rural colonization a grave mistake, because it would be difficult, if not impossible, to provide priests for the people scattered over the countryside. Cf. Maynard, *Story*, pp. 448 f.; Agnes C. Schroll, O.S.B., *The Social Thought of John Lancaster Spalding* (Washington, D.C.: Catholic University, 1944), pp. 210–213.

137. James P. Shannon, "Archbishop Ireland Colonizes," in Law-

rence M. Brings (ed.), *Minnesota Heritage* (Minneapolis: Denison, 1960), pp. 132–136.

138. James P. Shannon, *Catholic Colonization on the Western Frontier* (New Haven: Yale, 1957), ch. 7 and p. 267.

139. Theodore Maynard, *The Catholic Church and the American Idea*, (New York: Appleton-Century-Crofts, 1953), p. 278.

140. Paul Sultan, *Labor Economics* (New York: Holt, 1957), pp. 106 f.

141. John L. Spalding, *The Religious Mission of the Irish People and Catholic Colonization* (New York: Catholic Publication, 1880), p. 127.

142. *The Catholic Review* (March, 1881), p. 182 (all quotations in this and the preceding footnote are based on Schroll, *Spalding*, p. 118.

143. Maynard, *Catholic Church*, p. 278.

144. Aaron I. Abell, *American Catholicism and Social Action: A Search for Social Justice 1865–1950* (Garden City, N.Y.: Hanover, 1960), p. 62.

145. *Ibid.*

146. Cf. Henry Browne, *The Catholic Church and the Knights of Labor* (Washington, D.C.: Catholic University, 1949), pp. 238 f., 365–378. In a footnote to the text of his *Memorial*, published in volume I of his *A Retrospect of Fifty Years* (Baltimore: Murphy, 1916), p. 190, Cardinal Gibbons acknowledges "the valuable aid of the venerable Archbishop Ireland, of St. Paul, and of the Rt. Rev. Bishop Keane, who were then in Rome."

147. Henry E. Manning, *The Dignity and Rights of Labor* (London: Burns, Oates & Washbourne, 1934).

148. Cf. McEntee, *Social Catholic Movement*, p. 263.

149. Paul Jostock, *Die Sozialen Rundschreiben . . . mit Erläuterungen* (Freiburg: Herder, 1948), p. 6. Dr. Jostock, who recently retired as president of the Bureau of the Census of Württemberg-Baden, is not only one of the foremost lay leaders in the German Catholic social movement, but also a noted statistician.

150. The writer is in the following utilizing some of his own articles written on the occasion of the sixtieth anniversary of *Rerum novarum* in *Social Justice Review*, 44 (1951), esp. no. 3, 4–5.

151. Calvez and Perrin, *The Church*, p. 79; also C. D. Plater, S.J., *Catholic Social Work in Germany* (St. Louis, Herder, 1909); McEntee, *Social Catholic Movement*, pp. 34, 86 f., 263; Parker T. Moon, *The Labor Problem and the Social Catholic Movement in France* (New York: Macmillan, 1921), pp. 139, 158 f.; T. Brauer, "Der Deutsche Katholizismus und die soziale Entwicklung des kapitalistischen Zeitalters," *Archiv für Rechts- and Wirtschaftsphilosophie*, 24, pp. 209–254; Karl Waninger, *Der soziale Katholizismus in England* (München-Gladbach: Volksverein, 1913), p. 63; Francesco S. Nitti, *Catholic Socialism* (New York: Macmillan, 1895), p. 373; Paul Jostock, *Der Deutsche Katholizismus und die Überwindung des Kapitalismus* (Regensburg: Pustet, 1932), p. 118.

152. For this and the following paragraphs I am indebted to A. M. Knoll, *Der soziale Gedanke*, pp. 39–185, and K. Lugmayer, *Urkunden*

zum *Arbeiterrundschreiben Leos XIII* (Vienna: Typographische Anstalt, 1927).

153. Cf. Franz Müller (Franz H. Mueller), *Franz Hitze und sein Werk* (Hamburg: Hanseatische, 1928).

154. Cf. J. Albertus, *Die sozialpolitische Bedeutung und Wirksamkeit des heiligen Vaters Leo XIII* (Paderborn: Schöningh, 1888); W. Schwer, *Papst Leo XIII* (Freiburg: Herder, 1923).

155. Cf. T. Brauer, *The Catholic Social Movement in Germany* (Oxford: Catholic Social Guild, 1932), pp. 30 f.

156. Moon, *Labor Problem*, p. 63.

157. *Encyclopaedia of the Social Sciences* (1st ed.), 12, 74a.

158. Cf. H. Somerville, *Studies in the Catholic Social Movement* (London: Burns, Oates & Washbourne, 1933), p. 116; McEntee, *Social Catholic Movement*, p. 250.

159. Lugmayer, *Urkunden*, pp. 21–25.

160. Somerville, *Studies*, p. 85.

161. A. Lehmkuhl, S.J., *Arbeitsvertrag und Streik* (Freiburg: Herder, 1904), pp. 3–38.

162. *Rheinischer Merkur* (May 18, 1951).

163. Cf. Charles Comte, *Le Cardinal Mermillod* (Paris: Bloud & Gay, 1924), ch. IX.

164. K. Lugmayer, *Grundrisse zur neuen Gesellschaft*, pp. 34–36, 44–47. The text quoted above has been somewhat condensed and adapted.

165. *Social Order*, (May, 1951), p. 196a.

166. The picture of a "gradually veering" pope, recently used by an eminent Catholic historian of social thought and social movements is certainly somewhat unusual. It is quite obvious that here the wish was the father to the thought.

167. Cf. Waldemar Gurian, *Die politischen und sozialen Ideen des französischen Katholizismus 1789–1914* (München-Gladbach: Volksvereins, 1928), pp. 283 ff.

168. Lewis Watt, S.J., *Catholic Social Principles* (Cincinnati: Benziger, 1930), pp. 85, 76, 86.

169. George Jarlot, S.J., "Les avant-projets de 'Rerum Novarum' et les 'Anciennes Corporations,' " *Nouvelle revue théologique*, 81 (1959), 67.

170. Gérard Dion, *Industrial Council Plan* (Social Thought, [Ottawa, Canada], series 8, 5; item 61, 16), p. 3.

171. James Gibbons, "Organized Labor," *Putnam's Monthly*, 3, 1 (October, 1907), 62.

172. Abell, *American Catholicism*, quotes some statements by Quigley which seem to disprove these claims. However, there are indications that the Christian Reform Society of Buffalo did try to start Catholic workingmen's societies.

173. "The Catholic Church and the Labor Movement," *Modern Monthly*, 7 (May, 1933), 228.

174. Mary H. Fox, *Peter E. Dietz, Labor Priest* (Notre Dame, Ind.: Notre Dame, 1953).

175. In 1911, Dr. Frederick P. Kenkel, Director of the Central Bureau of the Catholic Central Verein, in a letter to Samuel Gompers, assured the dean of the American labor movement of the whole-

hearted support of the cause of organized labor by the German Catholic social movement of the United States; cf. M. Liguori Brophy, B.V.M., *The Social Thought of the German Roman Catholic Central Verein* (Washington, D.C.: Catholic University, 1941), pp. 74–76.

176. Cf. Edward Marciniak, "The Catholic Church and Labor," in Louis J. Putz, C.S.C. (ed.), *The Catholic Church, USA* (Chicago: Fides, 1956), p. 258.

177. Bernard C. Cronin, *Father Yorke and the Labor Movement in San Francisco, 1900–1910* (Washington, D.C.: Catholic University, 1943); Allen Raymond, *Waterfront Priest* (New York: Holt, 1955).

178. During World War II, Father O'Hea made a lecture tour through the United States and it is not unlikely that he shared his experience with prospective Catholic labor educators in this country.

179. Cf. M. D. R. Leys, *European Catholics and the Social Question* (Oxford: Catholic Social Guild, 1956), pp. 52 f.

180. John T. Ellis, *American Catholicism* (Chicago: University of Chicago, 1956), p. 106.

181. Cf. his article, "The Catholic Factor in the Social Justice Movement," in Thomas T. McAvoy, C.S.C. (ed.), *Roman Catholicism and the American Way of Life* (Notre Dame, Ind.: Notre Dame, 1960), p. 72 f.

182. Abell, *American Catholicism*, p. 106.

183. *Ibid.*, pp. 107 f.

184. *Ibid.*, pp. 109 f.

185. *Ibid.*, pp. 115 f.

186. *Ibid.*, p. 175.

187. For the whole preceding paragraph this writer relied on the article by Edwin E. Witte on labor legislation in the *Encyclopaedia of the Social Sciences* (1st ed.), 8, 657. Friedrich Baerwald in his *Fundamentals of Labor Economics* (New York: McMullen, 1947), p. 268, draws attention to the fact that in view of the rapid rise in earnings and standard of living, American workers themselves felt that wage rates were sufficiently high to allow them to take care of their own emergency needs. This attitude changed with the depression.

188. Cf. Ralph H. Bowen, *German Theories of the Corporative State* (New York: Whittlesey, 1947), pp. 75–118 (inaccurate in parts).

189. Quoted in Fritz Vigener, *Ketteler* (Munich: Oldenbourg, 1924), p. 542.

190. George Metlake (pen-name for J. J. Laux), *Christian Social Reform: Program Outlined by Its Pioneer W. E. Baron von Ketteler, Bishop of Mainz* (Philadelphia: Dolphin, 1923), pp. 180 f., 208.

191. Theodor Brauer, *Ketteler* (Hamburg: Hanseatische, 1927), p. 112.

192. Cf. Kurt F. Reinhardt, *Germany 2000 Years* (Milwaukee: Bruce, 1950), p. 617.

193. Since Ketteler died relatively soon after he began to espouse factory legislation, and shortly before Leo became pope, he could do little more than push open the door, as it were. Most of the practical work was done by Franz Hitze and his followers.

194. Maynard, *Catholic Church*, p. 277.

195. Published by J. C. B. Mohr, Tübingen, 1906.

196. "The Parish in the Rural Community," in C. J. Nuesse and T. J. Harte, C.SS.R. (eds.), *The Sociology of the Parish* (Milwaukee: Bruce, 1951), p. 102.

197. Cf. Coleman J. Barry, O.S.B., *The Catholic Church and German Americans* (Milwaukee: Bruce, 1953), p. 7.

198. Nuesse, *Social Thought*, p. 46.

199. *Ibid.*, p. 52.

200. Schroll, *Spalding*, p. 117.

201. None of the national pastorals until 1919 dealt with the social question or with labor problems. In 1852, there is a passing reference to the importance of the family for the security and prosperity of society; in 1884, the bishops speak of the "great social revolution" which is sweeping over the world; in the same year, they warn against secret labor organizations and repeat a similar warning made by the plenary council of 1866. Cf. Peter Guilday (ed.), *The National Pastorals of the American Hierarchy* (Washington, D.C.: NCWC, 1923), pp. 190, 252, 259, 262.

202. *The American Catholic Attitude on Child Labor Since 1891* (Washington, D.C.: Catholic University, 1938), pp. 46, 176.

203. Quoted *Ibid.*, p. 47.

204. Mary Elizabeth Dye, O.S.U., *By Their Fruits* (New York: Greenwich, 1960), p. 14.

205. McQuade, *Child Labor*, p. 45.

206. Dye, *By Their Fruits*, p. 15.

207. Patrick W. Gearty, *The Economic Thought of Monsignor John A. Ryan* (Washington, D.C.: Catholic University, 1953), p. 12.

208. *Ibid.*, p. 18.

209. *Ibid.*, p. 319.

210. *Ibid.*, pp. 24–26. Curiously, Oswald von Nell-Breuning, S.J., who was to become one of Germany's foremost Catholic social thinkers, chose the same topic for his Ph.D. dissertation. Cf. his *Börsenmoral* (supra note 12).

211. It speaks for Ryan's intellectual maturity and nobility of mind that he, who had grown up in an environment where (as he reports in his autobiography) Germans were regarded as "somewhat inferior" and the Irish as something like a "superior race," did not refuse to work with this rather German organization.

212. Cf. *Central-Blatt and Social Justice*, 2, 11 (February, 1910), 16.

213. *Ibid.*, 2, 1 (April, 1909), 9.

214. Albert Franz, *Der soziale Katholizismus in Deutschland bis zum Tode Kettelers* (München-Gladbach: Volksvereins, 1914), p. 221.

215. Cf. McQuade, *Child Labor*, pp. 86, 112, 121, 140; Abell, *American Catholicism*, p. 249.

216. *America*, (April 19, 1930), 42a.

217. Ryan, *Social Doctrine*, p. 44.

218. Max Scheler, *Nation und Weltanschauung* (Leipzig: Neue Geist, 1923), pp. 117–146. The article on militarism is part of this collection of articles published previously in various magazines.

219. Cf. Sombart, "Capitalism," pp. 206 f.

220. Cf. Clough and Cole, *Economic History*, pp. 723 ff.

221. *Ibid.*, pp. 766, 776 ff.

222. Bowen, *German Theories*, p. 171.

223. *Lehrbuch der Nationalökonomie*, IV (Freiburg: Herder, 1922), pp. 274 f.

224. Franz H. Mueller, *Economic Liberalism, Socialism, or Solidarism?* (St. Louis: Central Bureau, 1947), p. 22.

225. *The Economics of Heinrich Pesch* (New York: Holt, 1952), p. 180; cf. also Franz H. Mueller, *Heinrich Pesch and His Theory of Christian Solidarism* (St. Paul: St. Thomas, 1941), pp. 29–34.

226. Cf. Franz H. Mueller, Karl Heinz Brüls, and Albrecht Beckel, *Wer war Franz Hitze?* (Münster: Hitze Haus, 1959).

227. Müller, *Franz Hitze*, pp. 202 f.

228. Gearty, *John A. Ryan*, pp. 38 ff.

229. The publishers did a very poor job of condensing the text by simply omitting a number of paragraphs and thus destroying in several places the continuity of thought.

230. Raphael M. Huber, O.F.M.Conv. (ed.), *Our Bishops Speak* (Milwaukee: Bruce, 1952), pp. 243–260.

231. Cf. the bibliography in Mary L. Eberdt, C.H.M., and Gerald Schnepp, S.M., *Industrialism and the Popes* (New York: Kenedy, 1953), pp. 204–228.

232. Cf. *Central-Blatt and Social Justice*, 12, 1 (April, 1919), 2b; 12, 2 (May, 1919), 31a, 33a; 12, 3 (June, 1919), 66b.

233. *Ibid.*, 12, 12 (March, 1920), 381b.

234. Huber, *Our Bishops*, pp. 46–51.

235. *Ibid.*, pp. 50–51.

236. *American Catholicism*, pp. 189 ff.

237. In the roster of the Catholic Conference on Industrial Problems, initiated by the Social Action Department, the names of more conservative social reformers can be found. Frederick P. Kenkel, obviously, lent a willing and eager hand, here as well as in the rural life crusade of the department.

238. Huber, *Our Bishops*, p. 264.

239. *Ibid.*, pp. 272–300.

240. John M. Keynes, *Laissez-Faire and Communism* (New York: New Republic, 1926), pp. 1, 55.

241. Keynes, *Laissez-Faire* (for all quotations) pp. 59–61. "The theory of organization," says Boulding in his *Organizational Revolution*, p. 81, "points clearly to the type of organization which is most likely to be effective in the righting of wrongs and in developing progress toward the ideal. It should be 'polylithic' rather than monolithic, i.e., it should consist of 'many stones,' many quasi-independent organizations . . ."

242. Keynes, *Laissez-Faire*, p. 62.

243. *Ibid.*, p. 65.

244. Quoted from the third edition of his *Capitalism, Socialism, and Democracy* (New York: 1950), p. 416, in the *Review of Social Economy*, 19, p. 137. Schumpeter said that such reorganization would "presumably be possible only in Catholic societies or in societies where the Catholic Church is sufficiently strong."

245. *A New Social Philosophy* (Princeton, N.J.: Princeton University, 1937), p. 70. The late translator, professor emeritus of Oberlin College, who, though apparently a Protestant, used to work with the

Central Verein in pre-First World War days, reduced Sombart's enthusiastic statement to a mere "admirable."

246. Parker T. Moon, in his book on the social Catholic movement in France (Labor Problem, p. 340) has drawn attention to the fact that the Semaines sociales were not peculiar to France, and that the German social Catholics under Hitze's leadership had organized such social study courses and conferences since the 90s. For the Social Weeks in French Canada see the dissertation by Marie Agnes Gandreau, The Social Thought of French Canada (Washington, D.C.: Catholic University, 1946).

247. Austrian Catholics and the Social Question 1918–1933 (Gainesville, Fla.: University of Florida, 1959), pp. 68 f.

248. See Father von Nell's commentary on Quadragesimo anno, Reorganization of Social Economy (Milwaukee: Bruce, 1936), p. 269.

249. Drs. Brauer, Rommen and Mueller had to leave Germany after Hitler came to power and all joined, at different times, the faculty of the College of St. Thomas in St. Paul. Brauer died in St. Paul in 1942, Dr. Rommen later assumed a professorship at Georgetown University. Goetz Briefs is professor (emeritus) in labor economics at Georgetown University.

250. Gearty, John A. Ryan, p. 47.

251. Ibid., p. 294; Ryan, however, also drew attention to an important difference, namely the fact that N.R.A. did not provide for adequate participation by labor, consumers, and small businessmen.

252. John A. Ryan, Seven Troubled Years, 1930–1936 (Ann Arbor: Edwards, 1937), pp. 45 f.

253. Ibid., p. 161b.

254. Abell, American Catholicism, pp. 249 f.

255. "Degradation of the Family, Demoralization of the Youth and the Corruption of Business"; Statement of the Administrative Committee of the N.C.W.C. of November 15, 1933; cf. Huber, Our Bishops, p. 304.

256. Ibid., pp. 305–306. When speaking of what "the bishops say," we often mean the archbishops and bishops who form the Administrative Committee of the National Catholic Welfare Conference.

257. Ibid., p. 315.

258. Ibid., pp. 316 f.

259. Ibid., p. 317.

260. Ibid., pp. 317 f.

261. Ibid., p. 320 f.

262. Michael Chinigo (ed.), The Teachings of Pope Pius XII (London: Methuen, 1958), pp. 179 f.

263. Ibid., p. 299.

264. From the context (cf. the complete text published in 1939 by the National Catholic Welfare Conference, Washington, D.C., p. 19), it is evident that the Holy Father does not mean merely labor unions but all organizations of employers, employees, and farmers.

265. Chinigo, Pius XII, pp. 371 ff.

266. Huber, Our Bishops, pp. 324–343.

267. Ibid., p. 326.

268. Ibid., p. 329.

269. *Ibid.*, p. 330.
270. *Ibid.*, p. 331.
271. *Ibid.*, p. 332.
272. *Ibid.*, p. 333 f.
273. *Ibid.*, p. 335.
274. *Ibid.*, p. 336.
275. *Ibid.*, p. 334.
276. *Ibid.*, p. 337 f.; part IV of the bishops' statement as a whole rather than any specific passage or sentence demonstrates that the just wage is basically the economically correct wage and vice versa.
277. *Ibid.*, pp. 338 ff.
278. Chinigo, *Pius XII*, pp. 334 ff.
279. The word "unimaginative," while suggested by the context, is nevertheless not in the text, but has been inserted by the author of this article.
280. Chinigo, *Pius XII*, p. 335.
281. *Ibid.*, p. 336.
282. *Ibid.*, pp. 338 f.
283. More than ten years ago, when there was hardly any mention of underdeveloped countries, Pius XII spoke of nations "on an inferior or extremely low level of existence who, while taking a place in the family of nations beside their brothers who live in sufficiency or even abundance, wait in vain from one international conference to the other for a stable improvement of their plight." Cf. Address to the Sacred College, December 24, 1952.
284. Chinigo, *Pius XII*, pp. 316 f. (Radio Message to the World, September 1, 1943).
285. *Ibid.*, p. 345 (Address to the Christian Labor Associations of Italy, March 11, 1945).
286. Encyclical "On Promoting Catholic Missions" of June 2, 1951; N.C.W.C. edition, p. 21.
287. Chinigo, *Pius XII*, p. 86 (Address to the Sacred College, December 24, 1952).
288. *Ibid.*, p. 87.
289. *Ibid.*, p. 88.
290. *Ibid.*, p. 89.
291. *Ibid.*, p. 343 (Address on the Anniversary of the Christian Labor Unions of Italy, May 1, 1955).
292. *Guiding Principles of the Lay Apostolate* (Washington, D.C.: N.C.W.C. 1957), pp. 14 ff.
293. *Catholic Mind*, 57 (January/February, 1959), 83, 87.
294. *Ibid.*, 48 (February, 1950), 124.
295. Chinigo, *Pius XII*, p. 340.
296. *Catholic Mind*, 52 (February, 1954), 126.
297. *Ibid.*, 59 (November/December, 1961), 557.
298. *Ibid.*, p. 561.
299. *Ibid.*, p. 557.
300. *Ibid.*, p. 588.
301. *Ibid.*, p. 559. If the translation follows the original text literally, we can assume that Pius XII used the term "socialization" also as a synonym for nationalization. So in his address to the Christian Labor

153

Associations of Italy, March 11, 1945; cf. Chinigo, *Pius XII*, pp. 344 f.

302. Harbrecht and Berle, *Paraproprietal Society*. Cf. note 36.

303. W. H. Ferry, "Caught on the Horn of Plenty," *Bulletin of the Center for the Study of Democratic Institutions* (Santa Barbara), January, 1962.

Index